contemporary BOSTON architects

E. Ashley Rooney
With Gary Johnson
& Maryann Thompson

Schiffer Publishing Ltd
4880 Lower Valley Road • Atglen, PA 19310

Other Schiffer Books by the Author:
Boston: Past & Present, 978-0-7643-3058-2, $24.99

Other Schiffer Books on Related Subjects:
100 Boston Painters, 978-0-7643-3976-9, $45.00

Library of Congress Control Number: 2012939776

Designed by Justin Watkinson & John Cheek
Type set in Eurostile LT Std/Humanst521 BT

ISBN: 978-0-7643-4221-9
Printed in China

Published by Schiffer Publishing, Ltd.
4880 Lower Valley Road
Atglen, PA 19310
Phone: (610) 593-1777; Fax: (610) 593-2002
E-mail: Info@schifferbooks.com

In Europe, Schiffer books are distributed by
Bushwood Books
6 Marksbury Ave.
Kew Gardens
Surrey TW9 4JF England
Phone: 44 (0) 20 8392 8585; Fax: 44 (0) 20 8392 9876
E-mail: info@bushwoodbooks.co.uk
Website: www.bushwoodbooks.co.uk

CREDITS

Cover: JLA (© Anton Grassl), Meyer & Meyer (Brick Buck), Jan Gleysteen (© 2011 Richard Mandelkorn), Charles Rose (John Linden), ZED (Eric Roth)

Back Cover: LDA (Sam Gray Photography), David Sharff Architet, PC; KMD (Eric Roth), Maryann Thompson (Chuck Choi)

Page 236: Photography by Eric Roth. Used with permission from Beautiful Homes® Magazine. © 2009 Meredith Corporation. All Rights Reserved.

Front Flap: Charles Rose (John Linden)

Back Flap: LDA (Richard Mandelkorn Photography)

Title Page: Maryann Thompson (Chuck Choi), KMD (Eric Roth), Finemann (John Horner), Jan Gleysteen Architects (©2011 Richard Mandelkorn Photography), SsD, KMD (Eric Roth), Eck/MacNeely Architects (Eric Roth)

Acknowledgments

The creative act never ceases to amaze me; each new book is a novel experience, an adventure, and a challenge. There is a reason why I selected the particular architects for this book to be the leading-edge architects of Greater Boston. They do classy work, look to the future, and watch their deadlines. They came highly recommended with Maryann Thompson, Marcus Gleysteen, and Debra LaPorte (Debra LaPorte Communications) suggesting several architects.

Gary Johnson, a principal at Cambridge Seven Associates, adds some phenomenal talent to this book. As can be seen in the "Foreword," he certainly knows Boston's architectural history and how to explain it to the layman. Maryann Thompson's work is frequently featured in the national media. She has some fascinating insights in the "Introduction" about our homes and their links to our lives and the work of today's New England architects.

This book is about Boston and its environs, so I asked several excellent local photographers to provide me with some of their images: Fran Gardino, Walter Harrington, D. Peter Lund, and Harry Taplin.

Contents

Preface

The Pilgrims settled in Plymouth in 1620; in 1630, John Winthrop and other Puritans obtained a royal charter from King Charles I for the Massachusetts Bay Colony, which would eventually dominate the area. Precursors of the American Revolution, the Boston Massacre and the Boston Tea Party took place in the narrow, crooked streets of Boston; then there was Paul Revere and his famous ride. The first shots were fired on the Lexington Common — on that same April morning the Americans fired back at the British in Concord — and so began the American Revolutionary War.

Massachusetts is the birthplace of public education and, as such, is the home to some of the oldest and most renowned institutions of higher learning. The first pieces of American literature and philosophy were produced here. To this day, New Englanders are famous for their fierce independence, drive, liberal tendencies, and dedication to education.

By the end of the eighteenth century, Boston was a bustling seaport with a booming economy. General prosperity, the citizens' devotion to public service, and their pursuit of culture combined to make the nineteenth century a true golden age. If Boston was not the center of the universe, which some believed, it was certainly the "Athens of America," given its many universities, colleges, and educational institutions.

Boston was the site of several firsts: the first public park, first public secondary school, first post office, first lighthouse, first mutual savings bank, first Civil War free black regiment, first subway, the first free public library, first telephone, first marathon — the list could go on and on.

Its architecture was and is well known. Architect H. H. Richardson initiated a new style of architecture called Richardsonian Romanesque when Boston's Trinity Church was completed in 1877. Richardsonian Romanesque buildings are made of heavy masonry that gives them an almost fortress-like appearance. Great examples of Shingle style houses can be readily found along the New England coastline, where this first truly American style originated in the late 1800s.

Boston is home to history, education, sports, temperamental weather, and families that have lived in the area for generations. Today, Boston and its environs is one of the busiest and most exciting spots in New England. It has its history, tradition, and a beautiful harbor. Although it has grown from a small village to a contemporary city, it still retains many historic buildings and diverse, cosmopolitan attractions. People continue to move here not only for work, but also to raise their families and, when they build their houses, they need architects.

Boston's architects have often been at the forefront of current design trends, and the city is home to a number of very successful architects and architectural firms. The following pages present the work of the leading-edge architects in the Greater Boston area.

FOREWORD

A Brief History of Residential Architecture in Greater Boston

Gary Johnson, AIA
Principal, Cambridge Seven Associates

Built for a family of Puritan immigrants from Yorkshire in England, the house has been home to eight generations of Fairbanks. Believed to be the oldest surviving timber frame house in North America, the house contains many of the original features and is open as a museum. *Courtesy of D. Peter Lund.*

In Dedham, Massachusetts, a short distance from downtown Boston, you can find the oldest surviving wood timber frame house in America. The Fairbanks House was built around 1636, and it is a beautiful house. Composed of two floors under a steeply pitched wood-shingled roof, with multi-paned windows and a number of smaller later additions, it is a cozy and modest looking structure by contemporary standards. In its day, this home was considered a luxuriant home, designed for one of Dedham Plantation's most successful citizen families (original spelling of the family name was "Fairebanke"). This house remains standing today as a testament to the spirit and determination of those early settlers and to their knowledge of building techniques brought to this country from their native lands. They knew how to build a strong, long-lasting house that would keep out the harsh Boston weather and maintain warmth around the hearth. These builders constructed a home of permanence using only the local materials available to them. They also built a house with design traits that we still strive for: excellent proportions, unique textures, and an array of materials that remain beautiful and familiar to us to this day. The determination to build homes of this quality, beauty, and permanence continues as the ideal of all residential architects.

Throughout the last two centuries, residential architecture has played an important role in the development of Boston's architectural community. The city's architects have often been at the forefront of current design trends, and Boston has produced a number of very successful architects and architectural firms. Many of these architects, as we will see, gained their earliest successes by designing homes that helped shape their individual thinking and beliefs. Some of these homes and the architects' stylistic approach have greatly influenced, and even created new, emerging residential design trends locally and nationally.

What is it about the home that draws these Boston architects, or any architect for that matter, to design houses? Is it the simple act of creating shelter, or is it more about discovering a creative expression for both client and architect? It is probably both. The design process for any home is a very personal journey. For many architects, it is a way to express their talent and individual design skills on that most basic of building types. Working with and for their client, they are encouraged to create a unique living environment that is at once a design statement and a real working, living, breathing home.

A residence is an understandable equation. We know that a house is composed of comfortable spaces for eating, socializing, and sleeping, but the home is also a physical expression of who we are. It is a place that provides us with refuge from the elements, and it often reveals the sense of style and socioeconomic status of its owner. What makes residential design so fascinating is the varied ways it can be expressed. Homes can be rich in detail, color, and ornamentation, or they can be simple, unadorned, and plain. Their design can be based on historic antecedents or be forward thinking. In short, there are as many design opportunities for a home, as there are individual homeowners. The fundamental quality of good residential design is to push beyond the current limits. Architects, throughout the ages, have continually experimented with new and unique forms, exploring technologies, and emerging fashions to find an architectural expression that simply feels right. The house offers the perfect canvas for this kind of design exploration.

Like the contemporary Boston architects featured in this book, there are several important Boston architects from the past that truly shaped residential design. Today, these individuals continue to be an inspiration and major influence on architects the world over. Although they practiced at varying times, we still refer to the homes they designed as masterpieces and stunning examples of architecture. Surely tastes have changed since these architects practiced their craft and economic times have varied wildly, but one thing has remained the same: each home showcases the architect's talent and ability to transform a house from the banal to the sublime through skillful manipulation of proportion, texture, materials, color, light, and sculptural forms. Their homes are beautiful, graceful, grand, and sometimes lavish, but it is the architect's unique and evocative approach to design that serves as a window for us into the history of residential architecture in Boston.

H. H. Richardson

Henry Hobson Richardson, who practiced in the city from the late 1860s until his death in 1886, may be one of the most important architects to have ever lived and worked in Boston. He studied at the Ecole des Beaux Arts in Paris and, throughout his short but prodigious life, he produced some of Boston's preeminent buildings and fine homes. Recognized for his distinctive and influential "Richardsonian Romanesque" style of architecture, he is best known for his use of massive stone-bearing walls, semicircular arches, and soaring interior spaces. His architectural style is instantly recognizable and continues to enchant designers to this day. In his own time, Richardson influenced many notable architects including Stanford White and Louis Sullivan.

Richardson designed Boston's Trinity Church, Austin Hall at Harvard, the Crane Library in Quincy, Massachusetts, and the Marshall Fields Building in Chicago. Throughout his career, Richardson also designed houses. In fact, there are over a dozen houses of historic architectural importance credited to him beginning in 1867 and continuing until his death in 1886.

Located in the center of 109 acres of conservation land, the Robert Treat Paine House (Stonehurst) is the only house in New England designed by H. H. Richardson that is open to the public. In 1866, Robert and Lydia Paine commissioned architect Gridley J. F. Bryant to build a Second Empire summerhouse in Waltham, Massachusetts. When their family outgrew that house, they met with architect H. H. Richardson and landscape architect F. L. Olmstead to plan relocating the 1866 house and designing a great addition, as well as landscaping the surrounding grounds. In the spring of 1885, Richardson supervised the construction of the addition while the family toured Europe. Incidentally, this enormous addition and renovation cost the Paines a mere $36,000! *Courtesy of D. Peter Lund.*

The Stoughton House in Cambridge, Massachusetts, (1882) is a charming collection of dormers, pitched roofs, chimneys, and arches, all meticulously crafted from wood shingles in the style that ultimately would be referred to as the "Shingle style." The home is beautifully detailed and sculpted with the architectural forms normally associated with his works of masonry and stone. It is a modest house in some ways, but one that conveys permanence and importance. Henry-Russell Hitchcock has described this home as "one of Richardson's most successful works" and "perhaps the best suburban wooden house in America."

The Glessner House in Chicago, built in 1887, is a home that uses stone and stone arches in Richardson's more typical "Romanesque" tradition. This ruggedly handsome building is generally considered one of the most significant residential designs of the nineteenth century. It is a large residence formed around a courtyard with the exterior walls pushed close to the streets to create a private interior court. The facade is composed of rough hewn granite laid in a strong horizontal pattern and paired with minimal ornamentation, except for carved capitals at the second floor windows. There are carved foliage patterns along the imposing, graceful entry arch. This home is a true estate. Today, it serves as a museum showcasing Richardson's work and the English and American arts and crafts collections of the Glessner family.

Like the Glessner House, many of Richardson's commissions were built for wealthy patrons. Among the best known homes are the Tuckerman residence in Washington, DC; the Sherman House in Newport, Rhode Island; and the Ames Gate Lodge, a building he designed for his most famous clients, the Ames family of Boston and North Easton, Massachusetts. Richardson's residential designs shaped the look and feel of some of America's largest private homes of the latter nineteenth century. His designs evoke an elegance of structure, bold geometric overlapping forms, and the expressive use of natural materials that endures to this day.

Stanford White

Architect Stanford White was a protégé of Richardson. White worked for Richardson in his Boston office during his early formative years, starting in 1872. White also met his future partner, Charles McKim, while apprenticing with Richardson. The firm McKim, Mead and White would soon become one of the most influential firms in American architectural history. While White's stylistic approach tended towards Renaissance Revival, he was also skilled at designing informal, smaller wood and Shingle style houses and buildings. White's work was impressive, and his firm was well known for the architectural elegance of each commission. The list of works by White and his firm are vast and include Madison Square Garden, the New York University Library, the Gorham Building, and the Tiffany Building. But it was the homes that he designed that set a new standard for architectural opulence in the gilded age of American history.

Rosecliff, in Newport, Rhode Island, was one of the Newport summer "cottages" designed by White for Mrs. Herman Oelrichs. Designed as a true palace, this home featured grand interior spaces for resplendent decorative motifs used inside and out, as well as highly refined interior spaces in the European tradition. White would go on to design other "cottages" in the Hudson River Valley and fine homes in Manhattan for the likes of the Astors and the Vanderbilts, all with a similar flair for grandeur.

White understood the dramatic theatre of houses; he knew that the arrival experience in the home's foyer set the tone for the expectations of the guest and owner alike. Fine period detailing, custom designed furnishings, fabrics, artwork, and superb spatial planning allowed the rooms of his houses to flow together seamlessly. Space for privacy and intimacy was provided where needed.

White's skill, though, extended beyond the grand mansions of the time. He is often credited with having a major influence on the popularity of the famous Shingle style of homes of the 1880s, which remain popular even by today's standards. Although he may not have practiced in Boston for much of his career, White's influence as a major architect of fine homes can, I believe, be traced to Boston and his early training there.

Royal Barry Wills

On the other end of the spectrum was an architect named Royal Barry Wills, who was firmly rooted in Boston from his birth there in 1885. Wills no doubt knew of Richardson's and White's works, but Wills approached his career as a purveyor of residential design from a completely different perspective. Wills took the humble Cape Cod style house, which was one of the earliest and most recognizable of housing forms built in New England, and developed it into a residential style that has become ubiquitous to the region. The "Cape" was essentially a four square house with a center entry hall, a stair to upstairs bedrooms, and one formal room to each side of the first floor entry hall. It had a steeply pitched gable roof, sometimes with dormers, and often a central chimney.

Royal Barry Wills took this seemingly simple housing style and refined it to create a romantic form of architecture in the cottage style. Through the skillful refinement of traditional wood details, a careful understanding of proportion and scale of each of the house's elements, and attention to planning the floor layout, he took an old form and created something new and fresh. The American public loved it.

His designs were typically slung low to the ground with roof cornice lines directly above elegantly

proportioned double hung wood windows. Each house was anchored to its site by an oversized chimney, which became a part of the home's charm and character. His ability to create beautifully organized and harmonious architecture with simple roof forms, carved wood moldings, clapboards of varying widths and textures, shingles, shutters, and small paned, double hung windows is a testament to why the Royal Barry Wills Cape has become a hallmark of residential design and an instantly recognizable style.

In 1938, Wills was invited to submit a design to a *Life* magazine competition that ultimately pitted him against three other contemporary architects of the day, including Frank Lloyd Wright. The competing architects were to design a home valued at $5,000 to $6,000. Wills won the competition, and the home was built in Edina, Wisconsin. This style that Wills perfected would go on to be a traditional home, preferred by many Americans, especially in the ever burgeoning suburbs.

During the post-World War II building phase, many Royal Barry Wills Cape Cod homes were built in the Town of Lexington. One neighborhood was laid out adjacent to the "proposed circumferential highway" that would become Route 128. The Cape Cod house below has a bowed roof line and corner quoins. *Courtesy of D. Peter Lund.*

Walter Gropius

The 1930s also saw a new era in architecture emerge in the Boston area. The modernist movement was in full development in Europe, and Walter Gropius, the founder of the famed Bauhaus in Germany, immigrated to the United States — Boston in particular — to escape the influence of Nazi Germany. At the same time, Marcel Breuer, one of Gropius' protégés at the Bauhaus, also arrived in Boston. The two men taught together at Harvard University's Graduate School of Design in Cambridge. They would remain in the United States for the rest of their lives, developing distinctive careers and architectural firms of note that would bring the "International Modernism" style of architecture to this country. Their influence on architecture and architectural education has been, and continues to, be profound.

While at Harvard, both Gropius and Breuer moved to Lincoln, Massachusetts, where they designed and built houses for themselves. These houses have become iconic for their "mid century modern" approaches. The homes were designed with flat roofs, stark materials, and crisp, machine-like detailing that lacked ornamentation of any kind. Yet they are homes that feel at ease in their rolling New England landscapes, amidst lush fields and handsome stonewalls. The aesthetic was very industrial and "machine made," which was a component of what the Bauhaus espoused. This style was fresh and no doubt controversial in staid Boston, but the homes endure today as early examples of

Built in 1938, the Gropius house was forward thinking. It combined the traditional elements of New England architecture — wood, brick, and fieldstone — with such innovative materials as glass block, California acoustic plaster, and chrome banisters, as these materials were rarely used in that time. The large plate glass windows bring the outdoors in, but also permit passive solar gain. The rainwater and snow drain-off the flat roof through a center pipe to a dry well. *Courtesy of D. Peter Lund*.

what we now commonly refer to as "modern." They are the New England equivalent and the embodiment of LeCobusier's famous quote, "a house is a machine for living in."

Gropius would later form The Architects Collaborative (TAC) in Cambridge. This firm would go on to produce a host of talented architects who, in turn, were influential designers for a whole new generation of architects. Many of the founders of TAC would eventually build their own homes in Lexington, Massachusetts, in a cluster development known as Moon Hill.

These homes, built in the early 1950s, also remain iconic for their adherence to the principals of minimalist modernism. Inexpensive to build but high on style, these homes are classics today, some sixty years after they were first built.

Breuer would also continue to design houses in the Boston area and beyond. His work includes the likes of the Whitney Museum in New York and the UNESCO Headquarters in Paris, but it was his houses — more than thirty-five of them — that would continue to shape his style and craft.

Philip Johnson

Philip Johnson studied under Marcel Breuer at Harvard. After completing his studies, he established his first architectural practice in Cambridge, Massachusetts, where, in 1942, he built his own house on Ash Street.

Johnson designed himself a courtyard house that started at the street edge as a fenced yard. In essence, it was a fence that transformed into a house. This house still stands today. Located on a small site outside of Harvard Square, it appears from the street to simply be a 10-foot tall fence. A door concealed within the fence leads to an inner courtyard where the fence transforms into glass walls, also ten feet tall. Minimal and unobtrusive, the house design was a bow/gesture to an intellectual community known for interesting fences that bordered large Colonial, Federalist, and Victorian properties. It was a radical design for the 1940s: minimal yet not too out of character (at least not as far as fences in Cambridge were concerned). This home would also provide a glimpse into the future when in 1949 Johnson would move to Connecticut and build his truly iconic all-glass house.

These six notable architects from our past lived, studied and practiced in Boston. There have been many other talented Boston architects who have traveled similar paths before and after these individuals. Today, the architects profiled in this book continue the tradition of quality and innovative home design in American cities and towns. They are leading the trend in contemporary residential architecture with new ideals based on sustainability, net zero energy, and energy-producing homes. Inevitably, these ideals, combined with the use of reclaimed, recycled, and renewable resources, will allow the architects of today and tomorrow to design homes we can hardly envision right now. It is this constant pursuit for innovative design that ensures each new home remains unique to its environment and owner, continuing the necessary exploration of a home as the "machine for living."

Boston's leading architects will no doubt continue this pursuit and subsequently propel the discourse on residential architecture far into the twenty-first century.

Gary Johnson, a senior partner at Cambridge Seven Associates (C7A), applies his versatility as an architect and urban designer to a wide range of projects. With a Masters from Harvard's Graduate School of Design and undergraduate degrees from the Rhode Island School of Design and Wentworth Institute of Technology, Mr. Johnson's interest in urban design is utilized on projects in the United States and abroad.

INTRODUCTION

The House in Transformation

Maryann Thompson, Principal,
Maryann Thompson Architects

Some of the most important works of modern architecture were houses: Corb's Villa Savoye, Villa Stein de Monzie, and La Maison de Jules; Mies' Farnesworth and Tugendhat houses; Loos' Moller and Muller houses, to name a few.

These houses were essays on modern life, as their creators argued that the older models were no longer suitable. In truth, the house is architecture's closest encounter with life. It is basic. This is how we eat, how we sleep, where we sit.

The idea that the house must be tailored to life generates new architectural scenarios. Early modern architecture was as much about new life as it was new technology.

Similarly, today's lifestyles are profoundly different from those that the early houses in New England and the early modern houses originally accommodated. We desire different kinds of spaces. Our kitchens, home work spaces, relationships to natural light and landscape, our relationships to technology and energy use, even our closets and the way they are manifested say something about the culture in which we live and the values we support. Because the house is so intimately tied to life, its manifestation becomes a mirror of who we are. As we change, the architectural forms and spaces in which we live innovate.

For instance, the relationship of the kitchen area to living spaces has radically transformed in the last twenty years as kitchens become the new living rooms of our day. A decrease in domestic servants (and servant quarters, with the resultant separation required) plus the new ideal that family life takes place around the kitchen has led to the typology of the "great room": the merged kitchen, living room, and dining room, which often opens to the adjacent landscape or yard for outdoor eating. This paradigm is a radical shift away from past models and reflects both the multitasking that modern families do (e.g., make food and set the table while relating to each other and to nature and, at the same time, doing homework) as well as concerns about nutrition and its role in the wellbeing of the family system. We are seeing a trend in residential construction to eliminate the living room altogether in favor of this large spanned multipurpose room.

The advent of the "great room" in residential architecture has been supported by our ability to handle larger spans than in the past. The use of steel in residential construction, with its capacity for large spans, has also allowed for a more open plan where space is continuous rather than discrete. Technology has allowed for bigger panes of glass to be created, replacing the small paned mullioned windows of the past and increasing the levels of natural light in our living spaces.

All conspire to allow for smaller homes to be comfortable. Large expanses of glass not only allow the interior to be filled with light, but also facilitate the depth of the "borrowed" landscape outside to create a sense of deep space. Large spans allow for the feeling of generous space inside, even if it is just in one main room. These advances in structure and technology, along with the cultural acceptance of the combined kitchen, dining, and living room, have supported a whole new movement of small or "tiny" homes. Smaller homes will probably be the wave of the future, and they should be. They promote intimacy both within the family and within their context, as they rely on external spaces to complete their program. Family intimacy has, and will, become more and more important as the social relationships are exported beyond the physical space of the room via the Internet. Smaller homes are also inherently more "green" since they not only use fewer resources in their construction, but they also often use less energy in their functioning.

The advances in structure, glass, and envelope technology over the past century have also inspired a range of formal and material investigations into the perceptual dissolution of the boundary between interior and exterior. This investigation has facilitated a strong connection to nature within the architectural expressions of the past century. The dissolved boundary between interior and exterior was one of the central tenants of modern architecture and is still appealing today. Many of the early modern houses, however, failed to create comfortable interior environments. This is largely because the large expanses of glass were often not operable and were not shaded from the southern- and western-facing sun. The connection to nature was purely visual, facilitated by a thermally sealed envelope, which often overheated and created too much glare.

Bringing the subject into a closer relationship with nature remains a valid ambition; however, it must be considered in broader terms. In addition, sustainability is often considered too narrowly. It is primarily considered in technological and ethical terms. We need to think of sustainability in experiential terms. It has the possibility of critically extending the modernist discourse of interior and exterior beyond visual criteria.

Today's thoughtful New England architects have learned to create overhangs at their large expanses of glass to shield the summer sun and to let in the winter sun and to use many operable windows to facilitate cross ventilation. The connection to nature goes beyond just the visual to allow for the actual workings of nature to shape architectural form in search of efficient climate control and the creation of thermally comfortable interior spaces. Similarly, passive solar siting strategies, if available on a site, can further this agenda; the house becomes more deeply rooted in its environment by responding to its climate. Passive heating and cooling methods help connect a building to a site through a more thermally reciprocal relationship. We anticipate a variable interior climate through engagement with natural elements such as light and airflow — creating a richer experience. All these strategies conspire to have a powerful impact on our perception of the seasons and attune us to changes in nature via changes in our environment, creating a strong sense of "place identity" in an increasingly placeless world.

House design is one of the oldest and richest idioms, adapting constantly to cultural transitions and becoming a lens into the deepest values of the lifestyles they support. As houses outnumber every other type of building, they are the most widely considered architectural problem. Shifts in the conception of the home can and have had large-scale societal impact. Forward-thinking architects, working with visionary clients, can employ the medium of the home to envision new ways of living in the world. Thoughtful design will continue to create a shift, not just in what our homes look like, but also a shift in the values embedded in how we live.

The designs featured in the following pages reflect a diverse array of work currently being done in New England as well as highlight many of the transitions we are experiencing today.

Maryann Thompson has been practicing architecture in the Boston area for twenty years. Her practice is based in Cambridge, where she is also on the faculty of Harvard's Graduate School of Design.

Leading-Edge Architects

Bechtel Frank Erickson Architects

Lexington, Massachusetts

Finding the delicate balance between artistic creativity and real-life function is a skill mastered by Bechtel Frank Erickson Architects. Our architectural firm, nestled in the heart of Lexington, Massachusetts, is composed of a unique group of individuals who make it a priority to place the interests of their clients first and foremost. Under the leadership of Gerry Frank and Bill Erickson, the firm is committed to integrating each client's perspective into every project, offering creative solutions that are both aesthetically pleasing and practical.

From our personal experience, we understand that the design and construction process can be challenging. We utilize excellent communication skills so that our clients can benefit from our experiences and remain empowered as the ultimate decision makers with regards to their own homes. Although there may be stylistic differences in our finished projects, they all share a fine attention to detail combined with inventive uses of a variety of materials and textures. Another common thread that runs through our work is in the consideration of outdoor spaces or rooms as extensions to the home's interiors; it is critical to view the house within a context, be it an existing neighborhood or with relationship to the landscape and unique site features.

Our firm values the collaboration with the project builder. In our office, our teams remain intact from beginning to end. Thus, the people working on the initial design are the same as those drawing the details, interfacing with local building authorities, and meeting with the owner and builder reviewing the construction progress until occupancy. There is a certain joy in the creation of a new or modified home that we work to maintain throughout the process. We believe that this good energy translates to a successful finished product.

FRESH START

This 1800s Newton home provided a wonderful setting for a couple, both married for the second time, to renovate and make as their own. The couple worked with Bechtel Frank Erickson Architects to create a home that suited each of their talents and interests individually and collectively as a couple. Their house is now a showcase for a wonderful contemporary art collection. The open floor plan accommodates their busy entertaining schedule. The main entry was opened to the three levels of the house, which provided natural light to the core of the building. It also allowed the team to eliminate a superfluous servant stair that ate up valuable square footage at each floor. *Courtesy of Peter Lewitt.*

The new entry way has a good deal of natural light received from the second floor. There are views of the stairs and balcony type openings into the stairwell. The stained oak entry floor has a red leather insert. The fireplace in the dining room has a surround of 1 ft. x 1 in. multi-colored ceramic tiles. Bookcases flank either side of the fireplace. *Courtesy of Peter Lewitt.*

This area was originally divided into two spaces. Bechtel Frank Erickson Architects eliminated the separating wall and raised the ceiling to create a well-proportioned living room. The existing fireplace was clad in stainless steel and granite. The raised hearth was extended to form a window seat. The stained red floor creates a warm glow throughout the space. *Courtesy of Peter Lewitt.*

The eat-in kitchen was designed for serious cooks. It has a concrete counter top at the cooking island, a concrete surround of the fireplace, a magnetized chalkboard and rail serving as the fireplace mantle, maple wood cabinets, and cork flooring for standing comfort. *Courtesy of Peter Lewitt.*

A half-bath on the ground floor was created using 1 in. square glass tiles for the floor, Vitracor (colored Plexiglas) for the wainscot, and a corner glass sink and countertop. The goal is to provide a bit of color and introduce some unusual materials. *Courtesy of Peter Lewitt.*

The master bath was designed with a separate water closet, free-standing jacuzzi tub, and glass shower for two. The flooring is a combination of three materials — polished concrete, limestone, and squares of "pebble" tiles — that create a varied texture. The counters are Corian, and the below counter drawers are painted wood. New windows were placed at the end wall in order to bring in as much natural light to the bathroom area as possible. *Courtesy of Peter Lewitt.*

A late 1800s carriage house stood on this site. Bechtel Frank Erickson Architects undertook a complete rebuild on top of the existing footprint of the house. Their goal was to retain some of the original structure's character while imbuing the home with contemporary characteristics, such as an open floor plan, the latest technology, a high efficiency mechanical system, and energy-efficient windows. *Courtesy of Peter Lewitt.*

The house is situated at the back of a large vertical stone ledge hill. Its exterior spaces work in harmony with the stone outcroppings and the significant grade changes. *Courtesy of Peter Lewitt.*

Seeking to create a welcoming feature inside the house, Bechtel Frank Erickson Architects enlarged the stairway by extending every other tread up to the first landing, providing a highly desired art display space. *Courtesy of Peter Lewitt.*

This view from the main entry looks into the dining area, living room, and the sun room beyond. The columns provide separation of the living and dining spaces yet keep the desired openness. *Courtesy of Peter Lewitt.*

Built-in window seats and bookcases surround the sizable fireplace in the living room. The media room and the kitchen pantry are in the background. *Courtesy of Peter Lewitt.*

This view into the kitchen is from the kitchen dining area with the pantry area beyond. Hickory floors, painted wood cabinets for ample storage, and a great deal of natural light are the highlights. *Courtesy of Peter Lewitt.*

The well-lit pantry has ample storage space. *Courtesy of Peter Lewitt.*

Working with the new roof lines, Bechtel Frank Erickson Architects transformed the master bedroom into a space with great character. A thick wall created at the window provides a window seat and significant storage space. *Courtesy of Peter Lewitt*.

A meld of fairly traditional floor and wall tiles, contemporary features, such as the all-glass shower and jacuzzi tub, and good natural light create the comfortable master bath. *Courtesy of Peter Lewitt*.

SECOND CHANCE

A developer c. 1997 created the former front main entrance. A primary goal for Bechtel Frank Erickson Architects was to do away with it and create some distinct curb appeal. *Courtesy of Peter Lewitt.*

Bechtel Frank Erickson Architects created an entry hall by reconfiguring the main staircase. A music room and the family's formal living room are off the main entry foyer. This style combines some of the original building's traditional features with a decidedly more contemporary feel. *Courtesy of Peter Lewitt.*

The newly renovated entry no longer has many of the offending features: the old front porch covering, the spindly columns, and glass block window. The original massing was trimmed, and a new covered porch was added to create a more reasonably scaled entry. *Courtesy of Peter Lewitt.*

The new staircase replaced the original metal handrails and balusters with a wood rail and balusters turned 45 degrees. The opening to the family's formal living room is seen beyond. *Courtesy of Peter Lewitt.*

This view into the dining area shows the kitchen with the media family room addition beyond. The spaces are newly configured with elements such as the porcelain floor tile, Shaker cherry wood cabinets, and granite counter tops. *Courtesy of Peter Lewitt.*

The new media room is an addition to the original structure. The focus here was to include state-of-the-art technology within a dramatic volume, which allowed for acoustics. This space is an intimate meeting room and game area compared to the more formal room off the entry hall. *Courtesy of Peter Lewitt.*

The media room addition is articulated as a pavilion to the larger main house. The exterior materials are fiber cement clapboard, panel, and trim. *Courtesy of Peter Lewitt.*

This plaque on the Boston Common shows Governor John Winthrop arriving at the Shawmut peninsula. In 1630, Winthrop and other Puritans had obtained a royal charter from King Charles I for the Massachusetts Bay Colony and pledged in the Cambridge Agreement to establish a new colony in New England.

Elected governor of Massachusetts by the Massachusetts Bay Company, Winthrop is famous for his "City on a Hill" sermon, made onboard the *Arbella*, the ship that brought him to the New World. In that sermon, he declared that the Puritan colonists immigrating to the New World were part of a special pact with God to create a holy community.

"Consider that we shall be as a City upon a Hill, the eyes of all people are upon us; so that if we shall deal falsely with our God in this work we have undertaken and so cause him to withdraw his present help from us, we shall be made a story and a byword through the world."

Unlike the Pilgrims who settled Plymouth, Massachusetts, in 1620, many of the Puritans had titles, property, and education; their leaders were well-educated scholars. Along with their money, furniture, and other worldly goods, they brought with them a vision of the future. As John Winthrop stated, they wanted their new colony to be a biblical witness, a "city on a hill," or an example of biblical righteousness in church and state to be admired by the world.

About ten years after the Pilgrims landed in Plymouth, Winthrop and his fellow Puritans arrived at Salem on June 22, 1630. During that summer, many became ill and died. Winthrop traveled along the coast to Charleston, Massachusetts, looking for a suitable site for a capital. There, Winthrop met the reclusive Rev. William Blaxton (modernized to Blackstone), the area's first English resident. Blackstone invited them to visit the Shawmut peninsula with its clear spring of water. The site provided potable water, good anchorage, and good defenses. *Courtesy of D. Peter Lund.*

Catalano Architects, Inc.

Boston, Massachusetts

My passion for residential architecture began in sixth grade when my friends and I built an elaborate tree house. This first "Shingle style" project led to summers working for a builder and then to architecture school at the Rhode Island School of Design (RISD).

Upon graduating from RISD, my education was put to practice working for the acclaimed Robert A. M. Stern. While working in New York, I got my first commission (from my parents) to design a coastal Maine summerhouse. When the house was completed, my mother, unbeknownst to me, submitted the project to *Metropolitan Home's* annual design competition — and it won! The award and the exposure provided me with the boost I needed to start my own practice.

Since my firm's inception in 1987, my work has embodied a contextually sensitive, traditional American architecture aesthetic. A recurring theme that drives many of my designs is the significance of family and friends and creating a gathering place to nurture these relationships. Since becoming LEED certified, my work has incorporated sustainable building practices with traditional craftsmanship and architectural design. Despite having a well honed/over-arching style, each project serves as a singular expression; clients involvement and an acute awareness of their specific sites drive the unique design.

Although my practice is best known for expansive Shingle style houses along the shores of Cape Cod, Martha's Vineyard, and Nantucket, and elegant suburban homes nestled into the landscapes of the Northeast, we also work with commercial and institutional clients creating environments such as churches, restaurant interiors, and multi-space theaters. My firm's work is marked by a special sensitivity to, and appreciation of, important and often historic contexts and architecture that enhances those settings.

MARION COASTAL HOME

The formal symmetry of this Shingle style retreat belies the casual nature of the spaces within this family home designed by Catalano Architects, Inc. *Brian Vanden Brink, Photographer © 2011.*

The casual atmosphere of the pool reflects the equally relaxed yet classic New England character of this coastal home. *Brian Vanden Brink, Photographer © 2011.*

The kitchen is the center of activity for most families, which is certainly the case here. The accomplished cook can serve his or her grateful family in an informal setting on the teak-topped island. *Brian Vanden Brink, Photographer © 2011.*

Take in a breathtaking view of a coastal inlet and, at the same time, carry on a conversation with your hosts as they work in the kitchen. *Brian Vanden Brink, Photographer © 2011.*

As seen from the kitchen, this family room is organized around the beach stone fireplace and affords a direct visual connection with the kitchen and breakfast area. Notice the attractive built-ins. *Brian Vanden Brink, Photographer © 2011.*

Reminiscent of the Japanese influence on the birth of the Shingle style, this staircase exploits the sun and views through a two-story window. *Brian Vanden Brink, Photographer © 2011.*

Stonehedge Farm is the quintessential New England estate with its painted clapboards, Connecticut River Valley fieldstone, and Vermont slate. *Brian Vanden Brink, Photographer © 2011.*

Fieldstone chimneys, cascading stair windows, and a shade pergola frame the outdoor living spaces. *Brian Vanden Brink, Photographer © 2011.*

This light-filled grand staircase frames one side of a two-story entry foyer. *Brian Vanden Brink, Photographer © 2011.*

The entry to this classically detailed dining room is through an archway with a hidden pocket door. *Photo © Eric Roth.*

This story-and-a-half sitting room in the master suite is flooded with light and overlooks the owner's sculpture garden. *Brian Vanden Brink, Photographer © 2011.*

SOUTH BAY, CAPE COD

Flanked by the tennis court and pool area, the courtyard is entered through a long drive that winds through a grove of specimen trees. *Photography by Eric Roth. Used with permission from Beautiful Homes® Magazine. © 2009 Meredith Corporation. All Rights Reserved.*

The pool overlooks the garden and screened porch, forming a private space in which to view the bay or watch the setting sun. *Photo © Eric Roth.*

This tranquil pool has a view of the adjacent bay over its waterfall edge. *Photography by Eric Roth. Used with permission from Beautiful Homes® Magazine. © 2009 Meredith Corporation. All Rights Reserved.*

With its vibrant contrast between the rich dark floors and the creamy casework and trim, this kitchen exudes a calmness. *Photo © Eric Roth.*

This room is sited to take advantage of the views, the sun, and the natural breezes while protecting its occupants from the occasional insects from the nearby marsh. *Photo © Eric Roth.*

Boston has the largest harbor in New England. From its inception, the port was crowded with brigs, sloops, and later clippers that tied up at its many wharves. Brick warehouses took care of the expanding trade with the East Indies, China, and along the American coast. Whaling and cod fishing also became lucrative industries. *Courtesy of D. Peter Lund.*

Charles Rose Architects Inc.

Somerville, Massachusetts

I view design as a collaborative, explorative, and investigative process. My studio works closely with each client to develop multiple concepts until we find a unique solution. Common to each project is a concern centered on the nuances of the site, the interior and exterior spaces, and a refined material palette that utilizes local resources. Our work challenges the assumption that New England houses must be historical in character. Our designs are equally at home on the North Shore or the Cape and Islands as in urban America. Because they are interlaced with the site, they reflect the surroundings.

I tend to craft sculptural forms, with planes and volumes that shape space and light. I may bend a wall or tip a roof to fit the spaces or the site more effectively. Alternatively, I may do this to create a visual surprise — a view or a modulation of light — as one circulates through the house; a home's interior can be as experiential as the exterior landscape, with the juxtaposition of materials enhancing the form inside and out. Dramatic roof planes either extend towards the sea or echo the topography, creating a variety of spaces, large and small, open and protected.

If you live in one of our homes, you will come to realize the function of the angular forms — what the studio refers to as "fractured geometries" — that define our work. You will understand how gracefully the spaces flow into one another and the quality of light orchestrated over time, winter to summer. You will understand the siting of the building and choreography of views. Everything is considered; everything is crafted.

JIB HOUSE

North terrace looking east. Granite terrace with inset glass panels lets light into the lower level. *Courtesy of John Linden.*

View of the lawn area from the south. The glass walls of the living room visually connect the protected yard and the Atlantic Ocean. *Courtesy of John Linden*.

View of the south terrace looking west. The open L-shaped plan forms a protected leeward yard and garden. *Courtesy of John Linden*.

View from the rocky shoreline of the north elevation. *Courtesy of John Linden*.

View from the shoreline looking east to the north and west elevations. *Courtesy of John Linden*.

Detail view from the northwest. *Courtesy of John Linden.*

View of the pool and west elevation looking north to the Atlantic Ocean. *Courtesy of John Linden.*

Sited on a fifty-foot bluff above Pleasant Bay, the south side of the house is terraced, allowing for views across the bay to the Atlantic Ocean. *Courtesy of John Linden*.

View of entry to main house looking south. The house and landscape are integrated to form a seamless transition from inside to outside. The glass walls of the entry hall allow the sea to beckon the visitor. *Courtesy of John Linden*.

View of the dining room from the southwest. The large copper roof provides deep overhangs to the south and west and, in concert with the wood and patinated stainless steel louver system, provides shading to the house's interior. *Courtesy of John Linden*.

Interior landscape looking east to the guest wing and entry stairs. The exterior features copper panels, cedar and fir siding, poured-in-place concrete, and fin ply panels. *Courtesy of John Linden*.

View of living area looking northwest. The interior spaces were created around the owner's art collection. *Courtesy of John Linden*.

View from the dining room looking north to the kitchen. The interior palette includes Jatoba wood, granite, pre-cast concrete, and patinated stainless steel. *Courtesy of John Linden*.

Exterior view looking northeast. The project is sited on a steep slope with views through the tree canopy north to Vineyard Sound. *Courtesy of Bruce Martin*.

View from the west. *Courtesy of Bruce Martin*.

View at east elevation showing the porch to the south and an outdoor shower to the north. The runoff from the roofs is collected and discharged through two roof scuppers. The exterior material palette includes exposed aggregate, concrete, pigmented concrete, copper cladding, cedar, and mahogany windows. *Courtesy of Bruce Martin*.

Detail of northwest corner looking south. *Courtesy of Bruce Martin*.

The eating and kitchen area offers an expansive view of the surrounding woodlands. A natural material palette — mahogany, teak, and cork — brings the environment inside and offers visitors an inviting place to reside. *Courtesy of Bruce Martin*.

The interior couples clean, modern lines with casual living. Built-in casework eliminates the need for freestanding casework, making efficient use of limited space. *Courtesy of Bruce Martin*.

Built in 1713, the Old State House is the oldest surviving public building in Boston, and the seat of the first elected legislature in the New World. A unicorn and a lion, symbols of the royal government in London, are on its east side. The originals were burned in a bonfire in 1776 when the Declaration of Independence was read from the balcony. When the Boston Historical Society restored the building to its historical appearance in 1882, they were returned to their original place. The American eagle was added — appropriately on the west side — at that time. Today, the building stands proudly among Boston's twenty-first century government buildings. *Courtesy of Walter Harrington*.

David Sharff Architect, P.C.

Medfield, Massachusetts

Building or transforming your home should be a collaborative process and should deliver a discerning design solution tailored to your needs. Since 1995, David Sharff Architect, P.C. has been implementing this approach in partnership with our clients to deliver award-winning designs for new homes, whole house renovations, additions, and interiors. Through the thoughtful integration of beauty and function, form, space, and material, we instill the feeling that while fresh, beautiful and new, antique or modern, "this feels like it has been here forever."

An early interest in art, history, and construction led David Sharff into the field of architecture. David launched his practice with a focus on detail-oriented residential design and home renovation. Today, his award-winning firm's designs can be seen enhancing neighborhoods throughout New England.

David holds both a BA and a MA of Architecture (1988) from Tulane University and has instructed design classes at the Boston Architectural Center. David is a registered architect in the Commonwealth of Massachusetts and a member of the American Institute of Architects (AIA). David's civic involvement includes chairing the Medfield, MA Historic District Commission and being a member of Medfield's Planning Board. David has been a member of the Boston Society of Architects (BSA), the Builders' Association of Greater Boston (BAGB), the National Association of the Remodeling Industry (NARI), and the Northeastern Sustainable Energy Association. (NESEA).

Our designed projects have been featured in *Design New England* and *New England Home* magazines, on Discovery Home Channel's *Houselift*, ABC's *Extreme Makeover*, and HGTV's *Bang for your Buck*.

Our extensive experience in residential architecture and interiors results in a sensitive integration of new and old. David Sharff Architect, P.C. offers a client-focused, relationship-driven approach to working with you to achieve architectural excellence, thoughtful transformations, and sensible designs based on how you live and use your home.

CONTEMPORARY IN THE WOODS

David Sharff was asked to update a plain ranch style home that had been built in the 1970s. The owners loved the location, nestled in the woods, overlooking a private pond. The thoughtful addition of twin "pagoda-lik" wings completely transforms the house, opening it up to the landscape. *Courtesy of Ron Bouley Photography.*

This screen porch pavilion features a clerestory roof to let in natural light. The corners of the square roof are left open to let in more light, creating interesting shadows. *Courtesy of Michael J. Lee Photography.*

The interior is clean and open, framing views to the pond. A slate floor and tongue and groove cedar ceiling reinforce the natural setting. *Courtesy of Michael J. Lee Photography.*

The master bath interior finishes feature large minimal tiles, river rock accents, and other natural looking materials to further blend this space with the outdoors, creating a soothing, contemporary oasis. *Courtesy of Michael J. Lee Photography*.

Large windows almost reach the deck of the soaking tub, allowing the homeowners to enjoy their secluded setting from the master bath. *Courtesy of Michael J. Lee Photography*.

A 3,000 square foot high-rise apartment unit was a blank slate for architect David Sharff to create a sophisticated yet whimsical home for the homeowner and his children. The large living room is designed around customized built-ins and a collection of modern artwork. The result is a warm and family friendly space that appeals to the homeowner's modern sensibilities. *Courtesy of Michael J. Lee Photography.*

The living room is all about the view. Sharff selected low sleek furnishings that take advantage of the wonderful wrap of windows. A whimsical chair dominates a play area for the children. *Courtesy of Michael J. Lee Photography.*

The new kitchen is a busy hub. It features a mix of elm veneer and white lacquer cabinetry that reinforces the mix of warm, natural, and modern elements, which Sharff was careful to integrate throughout the unit. *Courtesy of Michael J. Lee Photography*.

The breakfast area features sleek modern chairs, colorful stools, and a reclaimed tiger maple table. It opens to the terrace. *Courtesy of Michael J. Lee Photography*.

The foyer, which leads into the coatroom, features arched openings, slate floors, and custom cherry built-ins. *Courtesy of Michael J. Lee Photography*.

The boys' bedroom features custom maple built-ins, including desks, beds, and wardrobes. Sharff designed individual reading nooks in each bunk to make nightly reading fun! *Courtesy of Michael J. Lee Photography*.

Stone knobs (lower right) are playful accents against crisp, linear cabinets. *Courtesy of Michael J. Lee Photography*.

The architect focused on adding details and design elements such as custom garage doors, copper gutters and downspouts, moldings and trim, and custom lanterns. *Courtesy of Michael J. Lee Photography.*

SHINGLE STYLE COTTAGE

The owners of a small Cape style house in the Boston suburbs hired David Sharff to bring a new aesthetic vision to their home. Through the addition of a garage, family room, and second floor bedroom, along with the careful integration of interior and exterior details, the architect was able to transform a basic white clapboard house into a charming Shingle style cottage. *Courtesy of Michael J. Lee Photography.*

The covered entry porch features a bluestone floor, bead board ceiling, and paneled walls. It creates a warm welcome. *Courtesy of Michael J. Lee Photography*.

The front facade is well balanced. Several design elements like the stone chimney, gambrel roof line, and integrated porch are pulled together to form an interesting composition of Shingle style elements. *Courtesy of Michael J. Lee Photography*.

Walls were removed on the interior to create an open and sunny kitchen. The cottage aesthetic was carried throughout as well, particularly in the kitchen cabinetry. A breakfast bar separates the kitchen from dining area on one side, and a large professional range separates the mudroom on the other. *Courtesy of Michael J. Lee Photography*.

The family room, several steps down from the kitchen, has a higher ceiling, which permits transom windows and a beamed ceiling. A gas fireplace is nicely integrated into a custom built-in. *Courtesy of Michael J. Lee Photography*.

The side entry of the house leads into a compact mudroom featuring custom cherry cabinets. From here, one can look into the family room, which was carved out of existing garage space. *Courtesy of Michael J. Lee Photography.*

In 1906, a new bridge was built on the site of the original West Boston Bridge. It was renamed the Longfellow Bridge in honor of Henry Wadsworth Longfellow, but it is often referred to as the Salt and Pepper Shaker Bridge because the towers on the main piers resemble salt and pepper shakers. The 1893 Columbian Exposition inspired Architect Edmund M. Wheelwright's design, which was intended to rival the great European bridges with their towers and stonework. *Courtesy of Fran Gardino*.

Eck|MacNeely Architects

Boston, Massachusetts

Frank Lloyd Wright once said that every project should have style but not a style. What he meant was that the style should not be predetermined but instead result from the design process. It should include such elements as a close examination of the site and a thorough understanding of the homeowner's needs. It's absurd, for instance, to imagine that a New England "Salt Box" colonial makes any sense at all in Florida. That's because the environmental forces of harsh winters and stingy sun that shaped the New England example are entirely different than the humid air and ever-present sun of the South. In our interpretation of Wright's dictum, we like to say: "Don't start with a style, end with one."

Using that maxim as a starting point, our design process includes four simple and time tested principles: thoroughly examine the site or context of the project, define the plan by the way homeowners really live, provide pleasing and well proportioned exteriors, and use details that are consistent with the first three principles. All four principles are interconnected, and the best projects, ones with a genuine style, will be the result.

The projects we have presented here are good examples of how we judiciously use those principles for every project, large or small, urban or rural. There isn't enough space in this short essay to describe everything we did, but, as a partial example, "The Inside/Outside Pool" on Lake Sunapee, New Hampshire, involved the homeowner's desire to blur the distinction between inside and outside and to connect the pool addition intimately to the rest of the house. Using an operable large greenhouse-like expanse of glass over the pool and an odorless ionic water cleaning system satisfied those two desires. The unique style of the pool was defined, in part, by applying our second principle of listening to how the homeowner really wanted to live. These timeless principles will always produce a distinctive project.

THE INSIDE/OUTSIDE POOL

Eck|MacNeely Architects integrated the interior and exterior of this New Hampshire home using an expansive greenhouse-like structure with operable glass that spans the entire pool. *Photo © Eric Roth.*

An odorless water purifying system allows for an open and direct connection between an informal kitchen, the pool, and the rest of the house. *Photo © Eric Roth.*

A unique turquoise and dark blue tile map of Lake Sunapee on the pool floor is clearly visible from the second floor landing above. *Photo © Eric Roth.*

Child-friendly features, such as this spray fountain, are spread out around the pool deck. *Photo © Eric Roth.*

By partially tucking the pool house addition into the ground, Eck|MacNeely Architects prevented its height from overwhelming the existing house. *Photo © Eric Roth.*

LOFT WITH A HEARTH

In this project undertaken by Eck | MacNeely Architects, the kitchen serves as a central hearth-like focus for this open city loft. *Photo © Eric Roth.*

A large island of white marble and fumed walnut provides an informal preparation and sitting area. *Photo © Eric Roth.*

An elegant steel rail and maple staircase leading to the second floor complements the kitchen ceiling. *Photo © Eric Roth.*

A light steel frame that spans over the kitchen/ hearth below supports a small mezzanine with operable windows. *Photo © Eric Roth.*

For convenience, a small home office is positioned just next to the kitchen area. *Photo © Eric Roth.*

Even the cutting board was crafted to fit the customized built-in sink in the black concrete counter. *Photo © Eric Roth.*

Eck|MacNeely Architects designed the new pool house to blend seamlessly in style with the house, also designed by Eck|MacNeely Architects five years earlier. *Photo © Dan Cutrona.*

The main house, pool house, and driveway entry are all interconnected by the use of similar materials and shapes. *Photo © Dan Cutrona.*

A large expansive wood deck ties the main house, pool, and pool house together into one continuous area for family use. *Photo © Dan Cutrona.*

A partially covered porch provides an intimate shaded sitting area for pool viewing enjoyment. *Photo © Dan Cutrona.*

A small whirlpool and lounging area at the end of the pool deck is the perfect area for viewing sunsets. *Photo © Dan Cutrona.*

Boston's ancient streets were often paved with cobblestones brought up from the beaches. Folklore tells us that the cows wandering aimlessly about the town determined the winding narrow streets of Boston. The truth is probably that the topography and a lack of urban planning were the reasons that the streets were laid out in such a random manner. *Courtesy of D. Peter Lund*.

Feinmann, Inc.

Lexington, Massachusetts

Feinmann, Inc., a design-build firm, started by Peter Feinmann in 1987, consists of a talented assembly of architects, craftsmen, and designers. One might be skeptical that good design can be fostered in a traditionally construction-based design-build firm, but we have found this work environment conducive to just that. The intertwining of the "cultures" of design, carpentry, and business has kept our work creative in its conception, artful in its execution, yet grounded. The result of this collaboration has produced a long string of awards for designs that have made Feinmann one of the most successful and well-respected firms in the field. Our projects have been featured in the *Boston Globe Magazine*; *Renovation Trends*; *Better Homes and Gardens*; *Fine Home Building*; *Boston Home*; *Design New England*; *New England Home*; *Robb Report Luxury Homes*; *Qualified Remodeler*; *Boston Business Journal*; and *Journal of Light Construction*, as well as on NECN's *Dream House*.

So where does the design philosophy of a design-build firm reside when set amongst a group of individual architects? You might not recognize a "Feinmann" design since each of our projects are unique and differ from one another — and that lack of "branding" is both by choice and by circumstance. We work in New England, which "constrains" design because it tends to be conservative in its taste and respects the historical context of its environment. We've been around for a while now and have seen the heroic age of Bauhaus architecture, which debunked buildings clad in historic references, be debunked itself as inhuman and devoid of human scale. We've seen post-modern architecture come and go. We've seen the rise of the architect "fashionista," where being noticed is more important than being good: the "Dennis Rodman School of Architecture." We've seen clean modern evolve into "Rococo" modern. Today, we're back to square one, as we're now seeing intimations of a new heroic period of architecture based on "green design." So what's an architect to do?

The design philosophy that we subscribe to has elements of some of the above. Where we can, we design something that will get noticed: something that redefines our sensibilities. In general, though, we believe every design should strive to be an inspired and sensible conversation between the architect, client, building, site, and budget. We typically tell our clients, "We have two clients — you and your house — both of whom deserve respect." Good design skillfully arrives at a creative balance between these clients; it is an inspired negotiation and it is this artful negotiation, or dialogue, that is the true mark of architecture. It is the choreography of a dance that will take place throughout the life of this dialogue between occupant and house. Recognition of this dance, this dialogue, is the origin of Architecture with a capital "A" — and in a region so steeped in historic precedent and in a design/build context in which the house often already exists, the two clients already have a very strong voice and personality. Being able to choreograph an artful dance in this environment is, in our humble opinion, the art of architecture.

ASIAN INSPIRATION

The client wanted a multi-purpose addition to meet several needs: a functional yet spacious home office, a beautiful entry way into the home, and a serene sitting area. An off-handed remark about always wanting a traditional Japanese scholar study became the basis for the design by Feinmann Inc. The "Japanese" addition shows shoji-like, which acts as a welcoming beacon as dusk falls. Roof angles and wall cladding harmonize with the existing house. The low horizontal window gives a framed view of a specimen Japanese Maple as one sits to doff outside footwear before entering the living spaces. *Photography by John Horner.*

The "Potemkin" carport is located behind the screen wall's garage door. The rhythm and style of lighting fixtures at the exterior continue in the interior along the entry axis. The aesthetic of the fixtures reiterates both the interior and exterior shoji pattern. *Photography by John Horner.*

This view from the "Scholar Study" shows the juxtaposition of the Japanese shoji screens into the Kalwall exterior wall, a play on translucencies and framed views. The outside lattice structure continues the horizontal pattern of the walls. *Photography by John Horner.*

This view looks into the living room from the entry vestibule. Kalwall flanks the entry hall to the exterior side and shoji screens to the other. The extended, rhythmic procession stands in stark contrast to the abrupt entry experience of the original building. *Photography by John Horner*.

The study portion of the "Japanese Scholar Study," the idea that inspired the project, is seen here. The simplicity of the furnishings is in complete harmony with the notion of a serene, contemplative space. The ceiling treatment references traditional Japanese architecture as does the horizontal window placed low, seen at the extreme right beyond the shoji sliding door. *Photography by John Horner*.

Two stainless steel workstations topped with white Carrera marble float in the center of the kitchen, making a dramatic design statement. They are anchored by a floating ceiling, which provides excellent lighting while reconciling the sloping ceilings of the existing house above, now off-centered. In the foreground is the sky-lighted "spine," which demarks the route from kitchen to garden, where fresh herbs and produce are grown for the table. *Photography by John Horner*.

In this view, a glossy blue transparent Arclinea cabinet, which contains refrigerator units and tall pantry storage, provides a bold contrast to the otherwise muted surroundings. The library ladder at the side allows access to an extensive library of cookbooks. *Photography by John Horner*.

Feinmann Inc. was asked to design a sleek Italian-style kitchen for a Second Empire period house. The addition was conceived as a space whose contemporary elements — the horizontal window wall and sky-lighted spine — peek through the otherwise traditional walls enclosing the addition. *Photography by John Horner*.

METAMORPHOSIS OF A BUTLER'S KITCHEN

The existing kitchen was truly the servant space of this grand home, lacking fine finishes and generous workspaces. Feinmann's addition now integrates the kitchen into the other, more formal portions of the house. It provides ample counter space as well as in-kitchen seating. The counter at the sink projects into a bay window with period-appropriate mullions to provide spacious relief from the narrower section of the kitchen. The wall at the end of the island is detailed to provide a separate but combined kitchen and breakfast areas. Various colors of cabinetry (some light, some dark) and dark granite counter tops, which contrast with the light oak flooring, further contribute to the visual interest of the space. Above all, it was the design's success in creating separation without isolation that most pleased the client. *Photography by John Horner*.

A deep beam and columns now hold up the former end of the building, so the kitchen forms a distinct, yet integrated space. Essentially set into a long and narrow configuration, it is relieved by its continuity with the breakfast space and by its provision for more intimate social space at the island counter, allowing the cook to remain part of the conversation. *Photography by John Horner*.

A poorly executed modernizing of a stolid Victorian residence created awkwardly proportioned and difficult to furnish spaces. Feinmann Inc. restored the spatial "intentions" of the original and provided many details while creating a flow between the rooms, conducive to contemporary living. The extended porch element is the most striking feature of the exterior; it is wrapped around the side and rear to enclose more living space and resolve architecturally the gawky rear elevation of the original. The front facade was essentially restored, with detail being added to the center bay to enrich its public face. The original porch knee-wall was changed to a railing. The "triple crown" featured on the porch fascia was continued onto the wrap-addition. *Photography by John Horner*.

The inglenook helps restore the natural proportions of the interior without isolating spaces as in the original. The fireplace, which has a horizontal orientation in its "modernized" form, is restored with more Victorian sensibilities, with rich details and a gold-veined stone surround. *Photography by John Horner*.

This space, known affectionately as the "bowling alley," extends the existing rooms. The dining room, for example, retains its intimate dimensions for family meals but can seamlessly expand into the "bowling alley" to accommodate festive gatherings. *Photography by John Horner*.

The octagonal "gazebo" with its panoramic views adds a climax to the "tour de porch" promenade. It is a favorite gathering spot for the family. *Photography by John Horner*.

The family adamantly refused to let a television dominate this space. The chimney at the side was on the outside of the building before the renovation. This area, which is viewed from the other side of the inglenook from the living room, is part of the extended porch element architecturally. *Photography by John Horner*.

The rear deck, mirroring the "bowling alley" inside, encloses an extension of the basement that now contains a family room. The restoration completely transformed the facade from the austere and architecturally ravaged (by the earlier modernization) elevation to a more animated and attractive part of the house. *Photography by John Horner*.

Within the City of Cambridge, Harvard University is a small, self-contained community, enjoying ties with the outer world but ruled by rituals and codes of its own. The oldest institution of higher learning in the United States, it sees its goal as one of guiding and leading — not just to teach but to inspire. In 1986, it celebrated its 350th anniversary. Today, Harvard Square is one of the busiest and most exciting spots in New England. The heart of it is the university with all its history, tradition, and town and gown. Although the square has been transformed over the years from a sleepy village to a contemporary city, it retains its historic buildings and churches, its curvilinear streets laid out in the 1600s, and its student population with all the associated cosmopolitan attractions. *Courtesy of D. Peter Lund.*

Gleysteen Design

Cambridge, Massachusetts

Founded in 1996 by Marcus Gleysteen, AIA, and located on the Charles River in Cambridge, Massachusetts, Gleysteen Design specializes in the design of new single family homes, as well as the renovation and reconstruction of existing ones. Our focus is on solving problems that require thought, creativity, and passion for projects of any size, ranging from individual spaces to complete estates.

Our cultural landscape is not static, and it is certainly not uniform. Our work goes beyond traditional stylistic boundaries. We pursue design solutions that are relevant to personal desire and contemporary life. We create new, re-invent old, or build upon the established, as we develop new architecture suited to clients, time, and place. Practicing architecture in America affords us the choice to engage with regional history and style, or not, as context and opportunity dictate. We find inspiration and great design either way.

We pursue the architecture of domesticity in the design of primary homes for everyday living. Our houses address the myriad complexities of daily life without aesthetic concession or compromise. Stylistic identification of our homes, when necessary, arises comfortably and naturally from the solution of collective and individual cultural requirements, along with the accommodation of practical and personal needs.

The following houses reflect project-specific solutions to diverse and engaging problems. Our first project builds upon a familiar New England theme, the farmhouse and barn, within a historical rural setting. The second project gives a nod to a typical suburban context while moving in an independent direction. The third project transcends vernacular context and tradition entirely in pursuit of singular sculptural form, while the final project improves the energy efficiency of a mid-century house.

SANDY POND FARMHOUSE

As a renovation and new house hybrid designed by Gleysteen Design, this house has gone through a complete transformation in style, layout, massing, and feel. Nevertheless, its overall relationship to the land has remained unchanged. The careful and sensitive site design and orientation of the house by the original architect allowed for a very light touch to be used on the land.

The exterior style of the house is contextually appropriate, pulling from the vernacular forms and materials of the surrounding nineteenth and early twentieth century farmhouses. The house is divided into two parts, a white-shingled farmhouse containing the sleeping and office wing, and a red board and batten barn, which houses the primary living area, the studio, and the garage boards.

The kitchen and dining area beyond abut a wall of windows overlooking meadowland. The kitchen consists of two storage walls with counter space for secondary appliances. The cabinets are faced with Douglas Fir with white bronze hardware. The countertops are Carrara marble. The fifteen-foot-long island houses the sink and cook top and faces out on the surrounding view. *Photo by Matt Kalinowski.*

A massive bluestone and granite fireplace, bordered by a reclaimed granite column, dominates the living room. The space, united by Douglas Fir ceilings, extends to the informal dining area beyond.

The formal dining room anchors the western end of the great room, connected to the kitchen by a hallway beyond. A 57-pound, foot-wide black steel beam runs down the hallway to the kitchen and informal dining area. *Photo by Matt Kalinowski*.

The master bathroom contains a large, walk-in shower. The space also features two vessel sinks on a Douglas Fir base, and a separate water closet with a custom Douglas Fir barn door and stainless steel hardware.

OVERLOOK HOUSE

Gleysteen Design organized this LEED silver house around a small stair tower/atrium that separates the family living areas to the left from bedroom areas to the right. The main exterior material, clapboard, is used to skin a collection of small building masses that recall more traditional New England farmhouses and outbuildings. Corrugated aluminum siding is used to separate and define contiguous building elements. Large windows and broad sliding doors open to patios that terrace down to a secluded garden overlooking marshland.

The house is built upon an existing footprint, replacing a house that was too compromised, structurally, to renovate and re-use. Built sensibly from sustainable materials, the house embodies the best in effective building technology and energy use. The size of the first floor was limited by proximity to wetlands, resulting in a cantilevered second floor that shades terraces below.

The front of the house is flanked to the left by the breezeway, creating a courtyard that is unseen from the street. The front door opens to a foyer with a mudroom immediately to the left on the inside. The breezeway doors pivot to allow free passage to the garden beyond during warmer weather.

A two-story foyer, bridged by an upper hallway, steps up to the main living space. The living room beyond is shielded from the foyer and front door by the back of a fireplace surround.

The form of the house reflects the desire for light, spatial flow, and family interaction. Individual living and working spaces are arranged around a central hall and stair that light and unite the house.

The freestanding fireplace anchors the living room, creating a buffer to the stair hall and foyer beyond. A granite, plaster, and walnut surround encloses the highly efficient pre-fabricated unit. The insulated chimney flue is encased in Douglas Fir.

During the day, the juxtaposition of solid forms and glass frame magnificent views of the woods, boulders, and ocean. At night, the dematerialization of the glass reveals a more active relationship between volumes, surfaces, and color.

Secluded on a ridge overlooking the Atlantic Ocean, the site provided twelve acres of heavily wooded buffer to the surrounding context. The main living space and deck fly over sloping granite ledges. The curvilinear roof shields a curtain wall of triple glazed, heat-mirrored glass designed to withstand harsh coastal weather.

Sculptural roofs and structures animate a more orthodox modern facade. The zinc-coated copper shingles reflect the color of surrounding boulders and rock outcroppings. The careful placement of roof overhangs and mechanical shades, along with strategically placed operable windows, keeps the house cool. *Photo © Eric Roth.*

Beyond the front entrance curtain wall, slabs of live-edged maple step up and around two massive granite boulders to the living room. The far glass wall opens to the deck and the ocean beyond.

The living spaces are defined by the interaction of solid volumes with a matrix of glass planes. The curving ceilings, clad in either copper or aluminum leaf, run like inverted glaciers between mountains peaks. Planes, surfaces, and volumes are delineated through the active use of strong colors in combination. *Photo © Eric Roth.*

Both the rectilinear and generic nature of the existing house allowed for Gleysteen's unfettered re-invention. Using upgraded materials and re-composed configurations of windows and sliding doors, the exterior was transformed without changing its essential modernist character while making it extraordinarily energy efficient.

The original fireplace is clad with bluestone slabs buttressed by two salvaged granite barn columns. The painting over the fireplace is by painter Harvey Quaytman. The underside of the re-insulated roof is clad in Douglas Fir with a plaster soffit below housing most lighting and HVAC components.

A composed figure-ground relationship between plaster and wood defines all the spaces of the interior. A painting by Peter Goodale hangs on the far dining room wall.

Located on the Harvard University campus in Cambridge, Massachusetts, Memorial Hall is an imposing brick building in High Victorian Gothic style. A prominent focal point, the 195-foot-high Memorial Hall tower was erected in 1874. The lofty vaulted transept has black walnut paneling, two large stained glass windows, and twenty-eight marble tablets bearing the names of the Harvard alumni who died in the Civil War. Various alumni classes commissioned and installed the majority of the stained glass windows between 1879 and 1902. The artistic styles range from traditional European techniques to the innovative use of new glass forms first developed by John La Farge and Louis Comfort Tiffany. Today, Memorial Hall is a National Historic Landmark. *Courtesy of D. Peter Lund.*

Höweler + Yoon Architecture

Boston, Massachusetts

Our practice, Höweler+Yoon Architecture/MY Studio, is a multidisciplinary design firm operating in the space between architecture, art, and landscape. We believe in an embodied experience of architecture, seeing media as material and its effects as palpable elements of architectural speculation. While our work lies at the intersection of the conceptual and the corporeal, we are also committed to both the practice-of and prospects-for architecture. Engaged in projects of all scales, we are interested in the material realities and material effects of our work that test the interactions between constructs and the public at-large.

Our multidisciplinary projects include architecture, planning, interiors, installations, furniture, and other items. We embrace all scales as an opportunity to engage in design research and investigate the relationship between form/performance, interactivity/media, and inhabitation/event. From concept to construct, from the big idea to the smallest detail, we are determined to realize projects of every scale and test them in the real world with real budgets and real constraints.

BRIDGE HOUSE

The directional quality of the house's three volumetric elements produces a linear connection between the suburban street and the views beyond.

The composition of rectilinear elements allows each to remain legible while providing facade articulation.

Large spans of windows gather natural light and views to the surrounding landscape.

The interior living space maintains a minimal and open design, blurring the threshold between outside and inside.

With full glass walls, the void between the volumes frames views of the landscape while also allowing the natural surroundings to slip through the house visually uninterrupted.

The exterior facade appears to nestle into the hillside as it negotiates between the public realm of a park path and the private realm of the domestic living space.

As the public park path meanders throughout the private space, a glimpse of the living room hovering above can be seen.

Full floor-to-floor glass emphasizes the horizon and invites the distant landscape into the intimate space of an open bedroom.

The use of horizontal wooden panels helps to articulate the continuous surface throughout the house.

OUTSIDE-IN LOFT

Open living and study areas allow for daily activities and interactions to occur seamlessly while also providing the flexibility to separate from one another through the use of sliding glass panels.

Located at the core of the loft, the courtyard acts as a light well, bringing the open sky and its elements down into the surrounding living spaces.

Minimal and clean finishes in the kitchen help allow natural light from the exterior courtyard to freely spill into the space.

With acid-etched glass enclosures, bathroom spaces are softly illuminated from skylights that flood the area with natural light.

Everyone visits Boston's Public Garden. The legendary pedal-powered Swan Boats, which arrive each April, are one of its greatest attractions. Inspired supposedly by Wagner's "Lohengrin," the Swan Boats have been there since 1877. *Courtesy of Walter Harrington*.

H. P. Rovinelli Architects

Arlington, Massachusetts

When a new client steps in to my office and sits down with me to review initial sketches for a house, we are beginning something far beyond arranging a set of rooms or establishing a construction budget. We are setting out to realize a client's dream. This is always the case, even when the project is small or the funds modest. All of my clients carry within themselves deep associations with homes they have lived in during other parts of their lives, ideas about what a new home might look like and feel like, and aspirations for what this new home might provide them and what it might say about them. I, in turn, as their architect, bring my own set of associations, preferences, and desires. We will design this new home together, working toward what will become a shared vision.

This collaboration is at the heart of what I do every day. I love houses, and I love designing and renovating houses. Each project brings its own set of issues and challenges so that no two projects ever feel quite the same. A guesthouse takes its initial stylistic cues from the grand Arts and Crafts mansion on its grounds but opens itself in a modern manner to a splendid skyline view. A country house draws on the traditions of a local New England house building, but gains a rather English character drawn from the interests of my client. A house by the sea for a large family borrows the language of fishing shacks and local barns in a crisp, mid-century rendition.

I have been designing houses for more than twenty years. I have learned in those years to be flexible, diligent, and detail oriented. I have also learned to be open to the exceptional, the unexpected, and the surprising in every commission, for it is from such that the best of my work arises.

GUEST HOUSE WITH A VIEW

H. P. Rovinelli oriented this brick, stucco, and glass guesthouse, set on the grounds of an Arts and Crafts mansion, towards a magnificent view of a city skyline. A greenhouse sits to the side of the living room, fronting a magnificent rose garden. *Courtesy of Eric Roth.*

The living room has a soaring, open ceiling and double height glass walls. The room was designed for the owners' collection of mid-century classic furniture. *Courtesy of Eric Roth.*

A stairwell, leading to a loft overlooking the main living area, conceals storage beneath. Mirrored panels within the stair wall help enlarge the feeling of a narrow passage, as well as offer reflected views into the living and dining rooms. *Courtesy of Eric Roth.*

The structural beam, which supports the loft above the dining room, acts as a railing, offering a view to the rooms below and out through the glass to a garden. *Courtesy of Eric Roth.*

A small bathroom offers the opportunity to realize a bit of architectural fantasy, with obscured glass square windows set asymmetrically into the outside wall. White statuary marble walls and floors, as well as a large mirror, anchor a free-floating vanity cabinet. *Courtesy of Eric Roth.*

MEADOW RETREAT

A mile-long winding drive, beginning in deep forest and opening dramatically to a large, sunny meadow, leads to this large country house set upon a knoll with lovely pastoral views. H. P. Rovinelli designed the house with a rich array of materials: mahogany windows and doors, slate roofing, board and batten siding, and a magnificent hand-laid veneer of a local schist. *Courtesy of Peter Kucinski.*

Rock outcroppings mark the extent of the meadow in this view to the rear facade of the house, with its long glass walls, steep roofs, and stonewalls. A bluestone terrace and a tall screened room offer family spaces for the warm days of summer. *Courtesy of Peter Kucinski.*

The open wood trellis of the pool house roof filters the strong rays of the summer sun when the family gathers by the lap pool. *Courtesy of Peter Kucinski.*

A glimpse through a passageway in the adjoining carriage house to a set of Adirondack chairs, set upon the expansive rear lawn. *Courtesy of Peter Kucinski.*

A soaring living and dining room, with a stone fireplace at its center, forms the heart of this family house. All the windows, doors, and trim work are mahogany, while the structural rafters above are of select Douglas Fir. *Courtesy of Peter Kucinski*.

The owner is a man who loves to cook. The extra deep base cabinets and countertop, as well as the massive gas range, are specifically designed for both pleasure and function in the kitchen. *Courtesy of Peter Kucinski*.

A SEASIDE HOME

Set between what once was a farmer's meadow and a ragged coastline, H. P. Rovinelli designed this house to maximize the pleasures of both the warm summer sun and a northerly view to the ocean. *Courtesy of Brian Vanden Brink, photographer.*

The house is designed without a single exterior painted surface: copper, cedar, stone, and mahogany will withstand the weather and mellow with the passage of time. *Courtesy of Brian Vanden Brink, photographer.*

A path of bluestone marks the entrance to the house, with a view through expansive glass walls out to the sea beyond. *Courtesy of Brian Vanden Brink, photographer.*

A local craftsman carefully assembled the oversized stones of the central fireplace in the living room, with a sheet of glass at the rear of the firebox allowing views through to the screened room. *Courtesy of Brian Vanden Brink, photographer.*

A dramatic stair, its carriage cantilevered from a tall wall clad in mahogany panels, leads to the family bedrooms above, and, still higher, a tower room with views across the coast. *Courtesy of Brian Vanden Brink, photographer.*

Exposed Douglas Fir rafters line the ceiling of an upper hallway. Bedrooms to one side gain cross ventilation through the use of frameless glass transom windows above the mahogany doors. *Courtesy of Brian Vanden Brink, photographer.*

The family kitchen, with quarter-sawn fir custom cabinetry, has a breakfast room with lovely views out toward the sea. *Courtesy of Brian Vanden Brink, photographer.*

The statue of John F. Kennedy, the 35th President of the United States and the first Irish Catholic American president, is located in the West Wing Plaza of the State House. A gift from the people of the Commonwealth of Massachusetts, it was dedicated on May 29, 1990. *Courtesy of D. Peter Lund.*

Jan Gleysteen Architects

Wellesley, Massachusetts

Jan Gleysteen, AIA, practices in the suburbs of Boston designing fine custom homes, additions, and renovations inspired by the historic architecture of New England. Classicism influences our firm's designs, which employ balance, scale, proportion, and symmetry. Our residences are subtly harmonious with themselves and their surroundings. This is most evident in our roofscapes, which evoke a charming historic character by scaling down the apparent size of the house through varying levels of intersecting gables and dormers.

Many of our clients are young families moving from the city in search of more space, a yard, and a home that is not only tasteful but manageable. To achieve this, we begin every design with the kitchen as "the heart of the home," where food and drink unite family members. The kitchen is a sophisticated space that serves as the social hub of the home, providing state of the art cooking, entertaining, and a center of operations for the modern family. The second most important space is the mudroom, which functions as the everyday "front door" and processing center for the family with cubbies, closets, benches, and peg hooks. Our careful consideration of these spaces is essential to the elegant livability of our homes.

Jan Gleysteen's favorite form is the curve in the shape of arches, barrels, bows, and circles; such forms not only subconsciously relate to our own bodies, but also provide playful interactions, especially between rooms and within the exterior facades. These ideas together with our study of historic details allow our homes to provide, in the words of the Roman architect Vitrivius, "Commodity, Firmness, and Delight."

PERIOD PINWHEEL

Designed by Jan Glaysteen Architects, this "new old house" is an academic replication of the historic Greek Revival Style found throughout New England. The low roof ridge maintains a historic scale while a pinwheel arrangement of rotating gables disguises the home's true size. Boston's 2011 Bulfinch Awards awarded "Best Suburban Residence" to this thoughtful design. *Courtesy of Sam Gray*.

A spin-off of the traditional front porch, this custom pergola connects the family room to the outdoors. Generous windows underline this connection while maintaining the historic scale and detail of the Greek Revival style. *Courtesy of Sam Gray*.

Glass cabinets, warm wood tones, and contrasting cabinets bring sparkle and warmth to the solid and practical New England pantry. *Courtesy of Sam Gray*.

The entry resonates with historic detail and proportions. Leaded glass and authentic window shutters cast striking shadows across the period moldings. *Courtesy of Sam Gray*.

Symmetry and drama strike a delicate balance in this historically inspired family room. A three-sided mantle anchors the main living space as light from the upper windows brings the faithful period detailing into dramatic relief. *Courtesy of Sam Gray*.

A striking mantle perches atop Doric columns under a distinctive ceiling, while French doors connect the entire space to the rear yard. *Courtesy of Sam Gray*.

Master detailing and careful proportions give a sculptural quality to the overall massing with a touch of added drama at the front entry. © *2011 Richard Mandelkorn*.

This bright and airy gambrel designed by Jan Gleysteen Architects combines the grace of a larger home with the coziness of a more modest one. Designed for a young family moving from the city, this home was recognized with a Gold Award from the 2011 Prism Awards. © *2011 Richard Mandelkorn*.

Gentle curves impart a quiet elegance to the airy interiors where particular attention is given to human scale and movement through carefully proportioned spaces. © *2011 Richard Mandelkorn.*

Curved mirrors and polished hardware add sparkle and elegance to the spacious master bathroom. Custom vanities are carefully detailed to provide generous storage. © *2011 Richard Mandelkorn.*

Modern appliances and traditional details merge seamlessly in the kitchen. The coffered ceiling anchors the island while the arches at the hood and window echo its traditional flair. © *2011 Richard Mandelkorn.*

An intimate niche near the kitchen becomes the command center for communications and scheduling. Central location and ample storage offer an ideal workspace in the heart of the home. *© 2011 Richard Mandelkorn.*

As the practical, everyday entrance to the home, this mudroom is functional and welcoming. Custom storage neatly tucks under the stair and is supplemented by custom cubbies nearby. *© 2011 Richard Mandelkorn.*

The sculptural rear façade is a surprising contrast to the demure front façade. The interior spaces push into the rear yard to create a whimsical yet balanced composition. © *2011 Richard Mandelkorn*.

This classically styled Shingle residence subtly blends traditional New England styles to create a striking, functional, and distinctive residence. Jan Gleysteen Architects' carefully crafted residence was recognized with a Gold Award from the 2011 Prism Awards. © *2011 Richard Mandelkorn*.

Traditional wainscoting, classical columns, and oversized moldings effortlessly blend in the formal dining room. Supported by a butler's pantry and nearby kitchen, this dining room is well equipped to entertain. *© 2011 Richard Mandelkorn.*

Playful curves and oversized classical elements create a dramatic family room. Vaulted ceilings and large windows bring garden views and natural light into the family gathering place just off the kitchen. *© 2011 Richard Mandelkorn.*

Contemporary and traditional meet in this thoughtfully planned kitchen. As the social hub of the home, this kitchen is designed to be the center of daily family life as well an entertainment center for guests. *© 2011 Richard Mandelkorn*.

Mahogany mantle and beams distinguish this comfortable library just off the family room. A crackling fire and rich wood detailing provide a welcome retreat from chilly New England winters. *© 2011 Richard Mandelkorn*.

The crisp and clean master bathroom is private and serene, a place to retreat from a hectic family life. The restrained palette and gentle curves lend elegance and tranquility to this private oasis. © *2011 Richard Mandelkorn*.

The Hancocks. *Courtesy of Walter Harrington*.

Jonathan Levi Architects

Boston, Massachusetts

Established in 1985 under the leadership of Jonathan Levi FAIA, Jonathan Levi Architects (JLA), is an architectural and interior design firm committed to the design of buildings and spaces that reinforce the highest aspirations of the clients we serve. The work draws its inspiration from spirited, collaborative inquiry with clients and exhaustive, energetic research into the full context of issues governing the individual project. JLA's projects respond to inherent opportunities directly and uniquely, through this rigorous method of design based upon the testing of alternative approaches. What remains consistent throughout the work is an economy of means and clarity of concept. In issuing them a recent international design award in housing, the juried panel cited JLA's approach as being aptly encapsulated as representing "an essay on values of clarity, simplicity and restraint that is timeless" and which "achieves a truly lyrical contemporaneity."

Jonathan Levi's approach to private residences strives to create forward looking spaces, including the most up to date innovations in technology and form-making while, at the same time, engendering qualities that make a home warm, inviting, and nurturing. The ultimate goal is to create places for living that evoke a sense of well being and belonging.

BROOKLINE TOWER

A paved bridge leads from the garage passage to the elevated front door. Minimal front-facing windows create an atmosphere of quiet privacy while at the same time guarding against the north winds.

The sun-filled south-facing living room opens to a wide-open valley view through a wall of operating custom glass doors. Plaster beams and a built-in, fourteen-foot upholstered banquette create an atmosphere of cozy warmth. The polished, poured concrete floor conceals embedded radiant heating for comfort and energy efficiency. © *Nick Wheeler*.

The tower-like form of this home designed by JLA maximizes view, light, and ventilation for each of the six levels while preserving precious garden space. At the rear garden facade, glass dominates in capturing abundant south light.

A rooftop retreat opens onto an adjoining terrace, offering refuge from the active family life below. © *Nick Wheeler*.

Created from custom-manufactured mahogany plywood with bronze flashing strips, the wood exterior surfaces emulate the permanence and dignity of stone masonry. The windows are also custom manufactured for ease of operation, maintenance, and maximum sight lines. All the glazed openings are fully operable.

HILLSIDE LIVING

JLA created a one-room-deep series of ground floor spaces set down the hilly site to create a unique sense of place for each household function. Fitted tightly to its gently sloped hillside, multi-level terraces and multi-faceted rooms maximize the interior connection to the outdoors.

The street appeal of the house relies on speckled brick and its intriguing walled courtyard.

A prized maple was preserved at the center of the house through careful coordination during construction. The tree flourishes today.

The garage structure is kept separate from the main house to create a breakfast courtyard in between.

The three-story atrium with bedroom balconies overlooks a yoga retreat on the roof.

The stepped living room culminates in the dining and fireplace alcove.

The dining room fireplace is shared with the front entryway. The operable floor-to-ceiling windows offer access to a mahogany deck.

The living level deck with corner glass doors offers a wide-open connection to the interior. © *Anton Grassl*.

FLOATING TREETOP HOUSE

A parking/drive bridge offers an innovative solution to car access to the hillside site. © *Anton Grassl*.

Specialty siding and custom windows create a tailored monolithic look.

The vertical volume of the main stair connects the lower entry and bedroom level to the raised living areas. The plaster casts are from the owner's collection. © *Anton Grassl*.

The overlapping dining, living, and kitchen areas provide a central presence for the gourmet cook owners. © *Anton Grassl*.

H. H. Richardson designed one of his most famous works, Trinity Church, in 1872 after the Great Boston Fire destroyed the first church. Completed in 1877, the church was one of the most ambitious church building projects in the nation. Built of Dedham granite and brownstone, the building is in the form of a Latin cross with a large central tower rising 211 feet on four huge piers. Shepley, Rutan and Coolidge designed the west porch and towers, which were added in 1897. Some have nicknamed the church "The Church of the Holy Bean-blowers" because of the giant angels with gilded trumpets at each corner of the roof. *Courtesy of Walter Harrington*.

Kelly Monnahan Design

Boston, Massachusetts

Kelly Monnahan Design's (KMD) "subversively modern" approach gives new meaning to private building. Whether urban loft, vineyard estate, or contemporary cape, each project is uniquely informed by site, environmental context, and the concepts of our time, with results that are at once profoundly familiar and wholly contemporary.

Established in 1999, Kelly Monnahan Design was the result of a three-year-long personal search for the perfect vacation home. Unable to find a suitable house, Kelly set about looking for land. Although designing a home from scratch seemed daunting, the process ultimately proved to be the most rewarding experience imaginable. Having worked at such Boston firms as Graham Gund, Shepley Bulfinch, and Sasaki, where his projects were always large, he found the intimate scale of a private residence to be liberating. The experience reminded him of what sparked his initial interest in architecture: he loves houses.

Kelly Monnahan is a nationally recognized designer who has dedicated more than twenty-five years to the field of architecture. Bringing an artist's perspective to the profession, Kelly pursues a relentlessly imaginative approach that unites clarity, precision, and restraint with a spirit of abundance. With an engineer's attention to detail and an architect's obsession for visual perfection, Kelly conjures spaces that are as beautiful as they are well-scaled.

With an undergraduate degree from the University of Oregon and a master's degree from the Southern California Institute of Architecture, Kelly commands an understanding of traditional architecture as well as the avant guard favored at SCI-Arc. The firm earned a BSA award in 2003 and was recognized, along with Keith LeBlanc Landscape Architecture, for a Boston Society of Landscape Architects (BSLA) award and an American Society of Landscape Architects (ASLA) award in 2010.

BACK BAY APARTMENT

For an art collector who wanted as much wall space as possible to display art, the decision to block windows overlooking Boston's Back Bay was difficult. As a compromise, KMD created moveable panels that can slide away behind walls to reveal the view from this penthouse apartment and that can display artworks. Primary partitions and large rectangular lava stone floor tiles are set at a five-degree angle to facilitate the concealment of building structure. The resulting forced perspective provides an enhanced view of the artwork. A Roy Lichtenstein painting presides over the living room seating while two oval Lucio Fontana sculptures from the '60s light up the dining room. *Courtesy of © Eric Roth.*

Floating walls help organize collections of art like the salon-style hanging of photographs seen beyond. A huge Murakami painting hangs between entrances to the two guest suites. The doors are full height panels trimmed in steel that slide out of the way to expand the gallery space. Photographs from Richard Prince hang over the bed. *Courtesy of © Eric Roth.*

Pin wheeling off the three main gallery halls are the family's private spaces. Ceiling recesses conceal mechanicals and lighting. A circular cutout allows an eleven-foot-high John Chamberlain sculpture to stand on axis with the west gallery, welcoming guests to the family room. Black and white portraits by Martin Kippenburger and Jeff Koons watch over the seating alcove. *Courtesy of © Eric Roth.*

The same Basaltina lava stone was used throughout the 8,000-square-foot apartment, including the master bathroom suite. Here, stone was custom cut in 1-inch-square tiles and set in a radial pattern, starting at the center of the Japanese style soaking tub. The Basaltina stone pillar conceals a structural column and provides a mounting location for the tub filler and shower head, both by Dorn Bracht. Sigmar Polke's black and white photographs complement the scale of the room. *Courtesy of © Eric Roth*.

The house is a modern take on traditional Cape Cod architecture, with a pitched roof, cedar shingles, and double-hung windows. *Courtesy of Keith LeBlanc.*

A 12-in.-thick wall protects the structure of the house on the northeast facade. The wall also becomes a parapet above, concealing a modern "widow's walk" along the length of the house. *Courtesy of Keith LeBlanc*.

Perched above the ground like a treehouse to take full advantage of summer breezes, an outdoor dining area can seat ten in a screened-in room. Lights are hidden above the cedar batten ceiling and the fourth wall incorporates an outdoor kitchen and grill. *Courtesy of Eric Roth*.

The entire upper floor is one large living space separated by a two-sided fireplace with the kitchen at the opposite end. The west living room wall is made entirely of glass windows that frame views to sunsets over Cape Cod Bay and Provincetown. The floors are Douglas Fir cut in ten-foot lengths and set in ten-foot bays to eliminate random end cuts in the open floor plan. *Courtesy of Eric Roth.*

A colonnade of steel columns, up-lit from the floor, march along one side of the house, delineating the circulation zone. An island separates the kitchen from the formal dining area and also serves as a buffet for entertaining. *Courtesy of Eric Roth.*

A "floating" angled wall organizes the open living space and creates a place to conceal media equipment. The desire to hide the TV in plain sight results in a design that looks more like a fireplace than a television. Guests have to look twice to notice the TV, especially when a digital fire is blazing on the screen. A Kasthall rug in wool and silk shag and a wall-to-wall drapery sheer, designed by Steven Sprouse for Knoll, make the large space feel intimate. The side chair is the Metropolitan chair by B&B Italia, and the encaustic on the mantel is "Untitled" by Keith LeBlanc. *Courtesy of Eric Roth.*

Like most lofts, there are no doors closing off spaces, with the exception of the bath and toilets. Rooms flow from one to the other, giving privacy and scale to each space. Careful planning ensures that the space doesn't feel big and empty. *Courtesy of Eric Roth.*

The office, an intimate space between the entrance hall and the dining room, can be closed off and used as a guest bedroom. Special lighting throughout the loft is seen here, slipping behind the lacquered wall panel and running up the side of the bookcase to illuminate the shelves. The dining room drapes are closed, creating an intimate experience. *Courtesy of Eric Roth*.

A wall painted with high gloss lacquer by Fine Paints of Europe reflects the light cast from the exposed bulbs of the Flos "Mod" chandelier. The wire frames of the B&B Italia chairs give way to the dramatic form of the Saarinen Tulip Table base. *Courtesy of Eric Roth*.

The chef's kitchen features dual Bosch dishwashers, subzero refrigeration, and a six-burner gas stove. A 4 x 12-foot stone island anchors the open kitchen and serves as a buffet table or bar for entertaining. *Courtesy of Keith LeBlanc*.

The sleeping area is hidden from view behind a 3/4 height kitchen wall. Openings into this area are staggered to allow light to penetrate deep into the dressing area while maintaining privacy from the public rooms. *Courtesy of Eric Roth*.

MANHATTAN MINI

In less than 500 square feet, this space is at the same time a cozy bedroom suite and a place to throw a party for twenty guests. The kitchen island makes for a perfect banquette table and bar, while the end of the "breakfast bed" by B&B Italia can double as a bench when entertaining. The floor-to-ceiling, wall-to-wall drapery by Creation Bauman acts as a giant lampshade, even at night, because of a tiny strip of LED lights running just behind the drapery track at the ceiling. *Courtesy of Eric Roth.*

Shifting the angle of the interior walls makes rooms feel larger because of the skewed perspective and helps hide unfortunate structural columns and chases. It also provides an opportunity to create hidden storage alcoves. The asymmetrical coffee table in matte graphite paint by Moroso contrasts beautifully with the high gloss lacquered ceilings by Fine Paints of Europe. *Courtesy of Eric Roth.*

The Boston skyline from the East. Note the Customs House Tower right in the center. The 1850 *Boston Almanac* describes the original Custom House building as: "Situated at the head of the dock between Long and Central Wharves, fronts east on the dock, west on India Street, and is in the form of a Greek Cross, [with] the opposite sides and ends being alike. It is 140 feet long north and south, 75 feet wide at the ends, and 95 feet through the centre…. It is built on about 3,000 piles, fully secured against decay; the construction throughout is fire proof and has the very best kind." The monolithic columns weighed forty-two tons each. Originally, the building had a glass dome. Today, a 495-foot classical revival style tower built in 1913-15, according to Peabody and Stearns' design, soars skyward. For more than thirty years the tallest building on the Boston skyline, the Custom House is a tangible reminder of the importance of the sea in Boston's history. *Courtesy of Fran Gardino*.

LDa Architecture & Interiors

Cambridge, Massachusetts

LDa's mission is to pursue design that improves the quality of life for our clients. We design collaboratively and follow a philosophy of "Finding Balance," seeking solutions that are at once creative, thoughtful, and inspirational, yet appropriately scaled, right for the budget, and comprehensively sustainable. We treat each project individually, resulting in homes where the architecture and interiors are a true reflection of the homeowner's lifestyle and lasting examples of quality residential design.

LDa is committed to sustainable design and has completed thirteen projects to LEED standards; more than half of our staff members are LEED accredited professionals. We have successfully demonstrated that we can create cost-effective and elegant solutions that balance design goals and work to preserve and enhance the environment.

Founded in 1992, our project experience is extensive, including both modest and expansive new homes, renovations and additions, interior design services, and sustainable design and consulting. As a successful New England firm, LDa has received numerous accolades, including awards from AIA New England, the Boston Society of Architects, and the American Institute of Architects. It has been featured in many local and national publications and books.

NEW AMERICAN HOME

Located in a quiet wooded neighborhood, this home was designed for a young family to reflect their active and creative spirit. The owners put a great deal of effort into the planning of the house and collaborated closely with LDa to create a program for contemporary American family living — meaning open space inside and out, natural light, and expansive views of the surrounding landscape. LDa designed the street facade of this dramatic waterfront site to be compatible in scale and height with the existing neighborhood. *Courtesy of Richard Mandelkorn Photography*.

The base of the house is finished in stucco, a reference to the turn-of-the-century home and carriage house that had occupied the site, while the second floor and roof are clad in red cedar shingles. This interesting contrast between smooth and rustic textures gives the house a formal, yet approachable quality. Bronze brackets visually support the broad roof overhangs. The rich composition of forms and materials creates a dramatic entry. The glazing at the sides and top of the stair tower brings natural light into all three levels of the house. *Courtesy of Richard Mandelkorn Photography*.

Outdoor rooms are as important as indoor rooms. French doors in the family room open onto a casual yet formal gathering space, which features an outdoor fireplace and stone patio. This exterior room benefits the most from the movement of the sun during all seasons. The scale of the home is intentionally low, permitting it to blend into the landscape. *Courtesy of Richard Mandelkorn Photography*.

The floor plan was designed to minimize wasted space; rooms flow into one another with no corridors, creating an efficient yet elegant open floor plan. The strategic placement of windows, views, and natural light helps guide one through the house. This view from the kitchen leads to the family room, to the library/dining room and finally to the second office. This room, located at the southern end of the home, can be closed off for privacy if needed. While the homeowners were drawn to a more traditional style for the home's exterior design, the innovative interior layout reflects the way that this modern family lives and works. *Courtesy of Richard Mandelkorn Photography*.

One of two home offices in the residence. This one, located next to the kitchen, acts as a command center for the family. The sliding doors create acoustic privacy while retaining visual transparency, as well as excellent views to the main stair, the back door and mudroom, and the kitchen. *Courtesy of Richard Mandelkorn Photography*.

At the fulcrum of the house, a "Jack and Jill" stair connects all three levels of the home and brings in abundant natural light, replacing the front and rear stairs found in a more traditional home. The blend of painted trim and naturally finished paneling lends this stair both a formal and informal quality. *Courtesy of Richard Mandelkorn Photography*.

ROCKY LEDGE

Designed to take advantage of the steeply sloping site, the home's full three-story height is only discovered as one moves to the ocean side of the property. Large groupings of traditional windows with transoms transform the shingled facade into a wall of glass, providing dramatic ocean views from almost anywhere in the house. *Courtesy of Sam Gray Photography.*

Traditional Shingle style roof-lines, and elements like the eyebrow window, further enhance the simple low massing. The atypical black trim and windows along with the broad arched entry feature were intended to set the house apart from its neighbors. *Courtesy of Sam Gray Photography.*

The blue stone terrace and "infinity edge" pool create the final transition from house to ocean. The terrace and simple landscaping featuring native waterfront plantings create a natural extension of the home into the rocky shoreline for relaxed outdoor entertaining. *Courtesy of Sam Gray Photography*.

The entry to the home showcases the striking use of black trim and details against the natural shingle siding. The curved arch and oval windows frame the custom bronze studded mahogany doors and one's first glimpse of the ocean views beyond. *Courtesy of Sam Gray Photography*.

The family room is centrally located within the entertaining section of the house and open to the kitchen and dining room. Molding and framing details are traditional in nature, but executed with a simple modern palette and style. *Courtesy of Sam Gray Photography*.

The entry foyer has an airy, expansive feel created by the full two-story height windows, grand staircase, and glass chandelier. The ebonized baked white oak floors are a sharp contrast to the white walls, a motif repeated throughout the home. *Courtesy of Sam Gray Photography*.

The client, a former fashion professional, inspired LDa to use New York and Paris apartments and men's suiting fabric as the basis for the interior color and material palette. This color scheme is spectacularly reflected in the library, with the use of black painted panel molding for the walls and a crisp white coffered ceiling. *Courtesy of Sam Gray Photography*.

The kitchen is compact yet richly detailed with a black marble top island and white quartzite counters. The layout is symmetrical: the oven and refrigerator flank each end, with the range and hood anchoring the center of the composition. *Courtesy of Sam Gray Photography*.

NEW ENGLAND CONTEMPORARY

The essence of this home, designed by LDa, was to explore the balance between traditional and contemporary forms to meet the separate desires of each spouse. The solution was to join two traditional New England residential wings together with a contemporary aluminum storefront wrapper. The seam between these two fundamental elements reveals the essence of the house and separates private and public spaces within. At dusk, the traditional windows speak to the intimate sense of privacy within the bedrooms while the curtain wall evokes the expansive nature of the cafe, dining room, and family room and the connection of inside and outside together. *Courtesy of Greg Premru (gregpremru.com)*.

The screened outdoor room with a stone fireplace and stained concrete floor acts as an extension of the family room. The wood and metal trellis joins the traditional and the contemporary together. *Courtesy of Greg Premru (gregpremru.com)*.

This kitchen was conceived as a collection of simple, monolithic forms of storage and fixtures that defer to the exposed structural system and the volume of the space. *Courtesy of Greg Premru (gregpremru.com)*.

The two traditional wings of the home are joined just to the left of the front entry. Here, a steel and glass two-story storefront system captures the space of the stair hall and provides a view through the "seam" of the house to the garden. *Courtesy of Greg Premru (gregpremru.com)*.

The exposed structural seam at the right marks the edge of the family room from the front entry and stair hall. A secondary structural system of glu-lam beams runs perpendicular to the steel seam to create greater height and volume. *Courtesy of Greg Premru (gregpremru.com).*

The exposed structural steel beam and columns join the private wings to the recycled steel stair, dining room, kitchen, and family room. A two-story glass wall brings abundant light into the space. *Courtesy of Greg Premru (gregpremru.com).*

In the early days of America, Boston's Back Bay was an inland bay. In 1890, it was filled in. The heart of Back Bay, Commonwealth Avenue is often compared to Parisian boulevards with its large grassy mall, statuary, and memorials. Its architect, Arthur Gilman, restricted the lots so that the houses were set back twenty feet from the property line. That step permits each house to have a small garden. Many Back Bay buildings are red brick and brownstone Queen Anne Revival. Gilman laid out the surrounding streets in a logical grid-like manner and named them alphabetically. This is one area in Boston where you won't get lost! *Courtesy of D. Peter Lund.*

Margolis Inc.

Beverly Farms, Massachusetts

Margolis Inc. was founded in 1994 to serve our growing repertoire of exclusive custom designed homes and renovations. Our firm specializes in intimately scaled projects of all types.

Originally from the Boston area, my training as an architect in both the midwest and west has broadened my international perspective of the natural and built environment. My master's thesis, "The Villa and the Garden, Suburbia Reexamined," reaffirmed my lifelong interest in domestic architecture.

Prior to establishing Margolis Inc., I worked as an urban designer for the renowned architectural and engineering firm Skidmore, Owings and Merrill, where I strengthened my awareness of proper land use and sensitivity to environmental planning.

Later, while working for Shepley Bulfinch Richardson and Abbott, I gained an additional breadth of knowledge in the rigors of classical proportioning, the relevance of architectural regionalism, and the significance of historical precedents. Today, as President of the New England Chapter of The Institute of Classical Architecture and Classical America, I continue to foster an appreciation of classical architecture.

At Margolis Inc., we are committed to offering client-sensitive design solutions that marry the built form and the landscape as a unity.

21ST CENTURY ARTS & CRAFTS

The northwest elevation at the pool terrace highlights the landscape design by Laura Gibson, ASLA. *Courtesy of Greg Premru Photography.*

The main porch on the home's west side overlooks the picturesque harbor. *Courtesy of Greg Premru Photography*.

Architectural ceiling details paired with soft, neutral colors in the living room offer a glimpse of the entry foyer beyond. *Courtesy of Greg Premru Photography*.

The dining room offers panoramic views of the harbor beyond. *Courtesy of Greg Premru Photography.*

Margolis detailed the custom millwork in the butler's pantry in twenty-first century Arts and Crafts style. *Courtesy of Greg Premru Photography.*

OCEANSIDE VILLA

Classical detailing shown in this south elevation is grounded with an ivy berm. *Courtesy of Greg Premru Photography*.

An exquisitely landscaped side terrace borders the Atlantic Ocean and takes its place as one of the jewels along Boston's North Shore Gold Coast. *Courtesy of Greg Premru Photography*.

An axial view peers through classical columns into the living area from the foyer. *Courtesy of Greg Premru Photography*.

Margolis Inc.'s seamless integration of the indoors and the outdoors is expressed in the living room with the landscaped lawn terrace bordering the exterior of floor-to-ceiling glass doors. *Courtesy of Greg Premru Photography*.

The Modern Movement inspired Margolis' renovation of this home. It includes a new kitchen and guest wing, a carport, and entry canopy. *Courtesy of Greg Premru Photography*.

The home's west elevation is shown here, featuring a newly landscaped terrace by Sudbury Design Group. *Courtesy of Greg Premru Photography*.

Privacy in the family area and guest suite is easily achieved with two 10-foot-square sliding etched glass partitions. *Courtesy of Greg Premru Photography*.

The new dining area looks toward the adjoining family room and guest suite. *Courtesy of Greg Premru Photography*.

On April 19, 1775, Major Pitcairn of His Majesty's Marines shouted at the armed Lexington militia facing him on that grey April morning, "Disperse. Throw down your arms, ye villains, ye rebels." Captain John Parker told the Lexington militia men, "Stand your ground; don't fire unless fired upon, but if they mean to have a war, let it begin here." The Battle of Lexington, which would begin the American Revolution, was about to begin. By the time the skirmish was over, eight Americans lay dead and nine were wounded. Standing on top of a granite boulder on the Lexington Green, the 8'6" bronze statue known as the Lexington Minute Man represents Captain John Parker, the leader of the Lexington militia men. *Courtesy of Eleanor Lund.*

Maryann Thompson Architects

Cambridge, Massachusetts

Integration builds successful design: during the process, in the finished product, and for the life of the home and its surrounding ecology. At Maryann Thompson Architects, we form a team among the owners, builders, consultants, and our own staff. Our design process is grounded in an ongoing dialogue and relationship with the site, our clients, and our team. Working with natural phenomena — shifting patterns of light and breezes, expansive views and sheltered nooks, delicate ecosystems and powerful landforms — our buildings find a solid foundation, energy stream, and inspiration for beauty. The end result is a house that grows out of the landscape, or cityscape, celebrating a series of moments from the connection with the surroundings to the private spaces sheltered within.

Our goal is to continue this integrative process throughout the life of the home. We invite light from above and cross-ventilation through each room. Weaving the languages of landscape and architecture, we dematerialize the boundary between interior and exterior. Our houses — indeed, all of our buildings — exist as an unfolding sequence of spatial experiences, each moment designed from the human perspective. Shifting effortlessly from the scale of the landscape to the detailed craft of building, our projects situate each resident and visitor dynamically within the materialized dreams of our clients. We love this process of weaving place and building, old and new, common sense and unique thoughts, for each home is a true expression of our client and another piece of who we are at Maryann Thompson Architects.

BLUFF HOUSE

Occupying the crest of a windblown bluff overlooking the Atlantic and nearby saltwater ponds, the house designed by Maryann Thompson Associates situates the occupant between an earthen stone plinth and light trapezoidal roof forms. Shifting and skewed roof planes simultaneously provide a sense of shelter and openness. The space between the planes allows for clerestory windows, which let in diffused light from above. Michael Van Valkenburgh Associates was the landscape architect on the project. *Courtesy of Steve Turner*.

Bluff House is a light-filled yet sun-sheltered four-bedroom home. The design for this summer home, with its wide overhangs and wooden interiors, is peaceful and shady, harkening back to earlier summer camps. The interior of the home shifts and turns to take advantage of light and views from differing positions on the site. Light from above, brought in through clerestory windows, gives the interior both a luminous and diffused shade quality, which is a welcome relief from the hot summer sun. The fireplace is clad in Vermont structural slate. It forms a central element in the house, addressing the sitting area, kitchen (on the left), and dining area (in the foreground). *Courtesy of Chuck Choi*.

The house both shelters the inhabitant from the summer sun yet remains visually open to enjoy a panorama of water views. This view from the dining area through the kitchen, with its window seat and beyond to the screened porch and distant landscape, shows the layered spatial quality of the house. The kitchen has a door that opens to the screened porch, allowing for easy transfer of food from the kitchen to the outdoor dining area on the porch. The screened porch is oversized, creating an indoor/ outdoor room with an ocean view. *Courtesy of Chuck Choi*.

The natural forms of the bluff generate the structure's complex form. The house visually becomes an extension of the landscape as the roof planes respond to the landscape and the cresting waves of the Atlantic below. *Courtesy of Steve Turner*.

A window seat nook near the fireplace addresses the distant pond view and is shielded from direct sun by a large overhang. Operable windows let in the ocean breezes. The cedar cladding of the roof underside creates a plane of continuity from inside to outside. *Courtesy of Chuck Choi*.

The angled floor plan allows for a sense of privacy within the neighborhood, blocking out the neighbors from view and creating a covered exterior sitting area facing the ocean. *Courtesy of Chuck Choi*.

Designed by Maryann Thompson Architects, this small vacation home rests upon an inland hilltop glade surrounded by conifers and native shrub grasses. The plan is divided between two volumes: the larger one contains the primary living spaces, bedrooms, and a study; the smaller one is designated as a guesthouse. *Courtesy of Chuck Choi*.

A screened "dogtrot" — an outdoor passageway between the two structures that provides shade and ventilation — simultaneously "joins" and "separates" the two spaces and opens the living areas to the outdoors. A pivot at the dogtrot folds the house at its entry. *Courtesy of Chuck Choi*.

The kitchen opens to the screened porch, extending the transitional space of the large screened porch and creating ambiguity between the inside and outside. *Courtesy of Chuck Choi.*

This view looks back from the screened porch through the kitchen and living/dining area. The dappled light entering the house through the trees of the wooded site gives a magical quality to the house's interior. The abundance of glazing in the house and its openness to light create a dialogue with the deep woods of the site. Its white interior becomes a canvas upon which the dappled light can play. *Courtesy of Chuck Choi.*

The tall ceiling heights downstairs hoist the bedrooms and study into the sky. Views from the second floor stair landing, master suite, study, and roof deck, which spans the dogtrot, disengage the occupant from the ground plane. *Courtesy of Chuck Choi.*

The site of this house is just off Long Island Sound, where it is strongly defined by the granite ridge that runs alongside it. Three distinct volumes reinforce the ridge line and nestle between existing mature copper beech trees. The house sets up a sequence of layers that contain and then release the occupant to the landscape. On approach, the west-facing public edge suggests an insular presence forming an entry court that veils the expansive view beyond. *Courtesy of Chuck Choi.*

Once inside, the building skin, which contained the occupant on the west, folds in on itself, transforming and opening up to the landscape and sun through broad expanses of glass and large sliding doors toward the east and south. *Courtesy of Chuck Choi.*

Existing stone retaining walls and foundations give form to the immediate landscape, dynamically etching the long history of this working farm. At times the middle ground is lost, hidden below the edge of the retaining wall, though linked directly with the far-off treetops of forest and the sound on the distant horizon. At other moments, clouds and fog isolate the site to its perch between the layered walls and the ridge. *Courtesy of Chuck Choi.*

Maryann Thompson Architects' undulating footprint defines a series of outdoor rooms that are spatially continuous with the interior. *Courtesy of Chuck Choi.*

Openings address unique views from or through the house to the property, creating a continual dialogue between the interior spaces and the pastures, nearby outbuildings, and the horizon. Here, the materiality of the stair walls, plaster mixed with marble dust, captures the reflection of the land, pulling it inside. *Courtesy of Chuck Choi.*

Fireplaces clad in dark ceramic tile anchor the distinct volumes. At the same time, they create defined layers of interior space that flows around and project the view past to the next space and out to the landscape. *Courtesy of Chuck Choi.*

The house unfolds in layers, culminating in unobstructed views of the farm and the ocean in the distance from a private balcony off the master bedroom. *Courtesy of Chuck Choi.*

North Bridge, also known as the Old North Bridge, is situated in Concord. Made famous by Emerson and Longfellow, the bridge is the site of the first American victory in the Revolutionary War. *Courtesy of Walter Harrington.*

Meyer & Meyer

Boston, Massachusetts

You might expect an architecture firm with a Boston Back Bay address to design in a classic style, but Meyer & Meyer brings out the timeless aspects of design, such as balance and proportion, which transcend styles. Our work encompasses diverse projects from a Georgian Revival manor to a modern penthouse in Greenwich Village, from a fanciful Hobbit-inspired retreat to a landmark Shingle style home.

At Meyer & Meyer, we approach each project with a fresh, imaginative eye and explore it from all angles. We capitalize on the drawing skills of our principal, John I. Meyer, Jr., AIA, LEED AP, to produce expressive, hand-drawn renderings, so our clients are guided directly into the excitement of the design process. Yes, we rely on computer-aided drawings and building documents too, but sketches and renderings help clients better visualize what a facade might look like or how a hallway arch might be shaped. These hand-drawn records often become treasured keepsakes for the client, charting the house's progress from idea to reality.

"We work hard with our clients to discover and refine the most beautiful expression of their values, their program, and their setting," says John Meyer. "We also work with dedicated craftsmen both locally and from the far corners of the world, relishing the collaboration that develops between the trades, designers, and the homeowner."

Extraordinary attention to detail characterizes Meyer & Meyer's work over the firm's thirty years in business. We offer and manage a full suite of services, from planning through interior design. Though the projects may vary in style and scale, we place the highest priority on client satisfaction.

"Clients want a close working relationship with their designers," notes Laura Brooks Meyer, IIDA. "They often refer to us as 'their' architect, as if we belong to them. We see it that way, too; we share their personal attachment to the project. We formalize their dream and become their 'inner architect.'"

The result is a uniquely customized home distinguished by elegance and serenity, in harmony with its site. Our homes are noted for their character and grace; they are designed to last for centuries and to be cherished for generations.

MAGNIFICENT CLASSIC

This 12,000-square-foot, Georgian-style home in Westchester County, New York, sits on a promontory and serves as the axis in a formal layout of English-style gardens. Terraces on the east and west sides of the house provide generous views and create harmony between house and landscape. The 85-acre estate includes a refreshing Moorish-style fountain. This home was presented with the Prism Gold Award for Best New Single Family Home over 5,000 square feet. © *Bedford Photo-Graphic, Inc.*

Elegant bronze doors hint at the grandeur that awaits within. The choice of metal also finds its complement in the staircase railing. The opulent and refined stylistic elements of the entire house reflect the influence of America's Gilded Age. The ornate moldings and statuesque columns are crowned with a coffered ceiling ,which is decorated in three types of gold leaf, making it gleam like a jewel box. *Courtesy of Bruce Buck*.

A striking sight, the staircase boasts custom-cut limestone treads and risers, as well as a new custom-made bronze railing and newel post that terminates in a flourish, with a column topped by dramatic lighting. The interiors reflect a French Rococo sensibility, in keeping with the client's preferences. John Canning Painting & Conservation Studios did the decorative painting found throughout the house. This home was presented with the Prism Gold Award for Best Remodeling/Restoration over $500,000 and with Dream Home's 2010 Home of the Year Award. *Courtesy of Bruce Buck*.

A piano provides a graceful note in the reception hall of this English estate. *Courtesy of Bruce Buck.*

ORCHARD BARN

The 2,800-square-foot Orchard Barn — named for its proximity to an apple orchard — provides space for large gatherings, recreation, and fundraising events. Its design uses solar power as a supplemental energy source. Photovoltaic panels were integrated into the overall design, so the barn is able to generate its own electricity. *Photo © Eric Roth*.

Sturdy, reclaimed, carved beams frame a cupola with an antique Fresnel lens. The lens was named after the early nineteenth-century French engineer who developed it. Fresnel lenses were frequently found in lighthouses because they were much larger, thinner, and flatter, and capable of capturing more oblique light. *Photo © Eric Roth*.

The custom-designed copper-topped bar features hand carvings in the English style and serves as the barn's hub. The barn also houses a full kitchen with elevator access to the second floor loft space, making entertaining convenient. *Photo © Eric Roth*.

Neatly tucked into the landscape, this children's warming hut sits quietly on a small island surrounded by three bodies of water: one for trout fishing, one for ice skating, and a natural reflecting pool. The fairytale aspect shows especially well at dusk, when lights from the windows are reflected in a pond edged by ornamental trees, plants, and stonework. Natural materials such as stone, slate, copper, and cedar give texture to the undulating forms of the roof-line and lidded dormer windows. © *Robert Benson Photography*.

The rustic hut features a southern facing stone terrace and outdoor fireplace overlooking the water. Architect John Meyer calls the structure "a cross between a miner shack and a hobbit hut." Its 1,800 square feet includes a family room, kitchen, bathroom, and a small office on the first floor.

Hand-carved in Budapest, this limestone fireplace is the focal point of the hut's interior. © *Robert Benson Photography*.

BEACHBAY POINT

Taking a fresh approach to waterfront Shingle style, this unique home designed by Meyer and Meyer treats every possible view with distinction. From the stone set gates to the undulating drive up the hill, one enjoys glimpses of the house and water upon approach. The custom hand-carved wood railing lends natural movement within the space. *Courtesy of Richard Mandelkorn*.

Fluid roof-lines and gracefully curved windows, set among cupolas and cedar shingles, flow with the water views and private grounds. No true front, back, or sides of this house exist. Rather, it follows the curves of the point to be appreciated from all angles. *Courtesy of Richard Mandelkorn*.

From the beach, this view catches a series of decks and accesses back to the house. One may cross a playful stone bridge to a terrace with an exterior fireplace or climb winding stairs to dining terraces to capture 270 degrees of sweeping water views. A stone jacuzzi is sheltered from breezes and becomes the forefront of views from inside the lower level recreation and entertainment rooms. *Courtesy of Richard Mandelkorn*.

Natural materials such as stone, carved timber, copper, and slate blend together under a covered portico entry. *Courtesy of Richard Mandelkorn*.

A three-car garage repeats the rhythm of subtle waves beyond with strength and grace. *Courtesy of Richard Mandelkorn*.

The detail of this custom designed entry door and hand blown glass sidelights gives way to the home's specialty features. *Courtesy of Richard Mandelkorn*.

The custom hand-carved wood railing lends natural movement within the space. *Courtesy of Richard Mandelkorn.*

The master bedroom's double doors open to a secluded deck, giving a sense of being at the helm of a private ship. *Courtesy of Richard Mandelkorn.*

The Royall House and Slave Quarters were built in 1732-1737. Isaac Royall brought his family and slaves from Antigua to Medford, Massachusetts. On the eve of the American Revolution, his son, despite his sympathies for the Patriots, sailed to Nova Scotia. A National Historic Landmark, the house is a fine eighteenth century building, and the slave quarters (right) are said to be the only such structure in the northern United States. *Courtesy of D. Peter Lund*

Moskow Linn Architects, Inc.

Boston, Massachusetts

Moskow Linn Architects, Inc. is a Boston-based firm committed to environmentally sensitive architecture. In practice since 1990, the firm has designed custom residences, institutional buildings, and master plans for future growth and strategic development in urban and rural areas.

Moskow Linn Architects, Inc. has been honored with national and regional awards for design excellence, specifically for their success in offering a memorable sense of place, one that is in harmony with both its occupants and the environment. The firm encourages client participation to create buildings that are responsive to their users and fit comfortably within their community.

Keith Moskow, FAIA, received a Bachelor of Arts from Dartmouth College and a Masters of Architecture from the University of Pennsylvania. He has received design awards from the American Institute of Architects, the Boston Society of Architects, and the Municipal Arts Society of New York. Keith is the Commissioner of Professional Practice for the Boston Society of Architects and is the author of four books on architecture.

Robert Linn received an undergraduate degree in architecture from the University of Arkansas and a Masters of Architecture from Harvard University. He has won awards from the American Society of Perspectivists, the American Institute of Architects, the Boston Society of Architects, and a gold medal in the Seoul Design Olympiad. Robert was a recipient of the Rotch Fellowship and is the author of two books on architecture.

MVII

PAGES 183-185: The house is composed of three elements: an arcade, a structure for sleeping, and a structure for living. The linear building components frame an outdoor court and align with a view corridor cut through the wilderness. All wood is exposed and left in its natural state. *Courtesy of © Eric Roth.*

ARBOR HOUSE

PAGES 186-187: This 800-square-foot house, designed by Moskow Linn Architects, includes a grape arbor that collects the living areas like a seine net, extending outward to create a courtyard. *Courtesy of Greg Premru (gregpremru.com)*.

RESERVOIR HOUSE

PAGES 188-189: The year-round house is engineered to rely solely on passive solar energy for heating and cooling. All furniture was custom designed for the residence. *Courtesy of Greg Premru (gregpremru.com)*.

RICE ISLAND HOUSE

PAGES 190-191: This extensive renovation, designed by Moskow Linn Architects, allows the house to engage its unique coastal site. Its character was derived from an amalgam of New England architecture and the owner's interest in boats. *Courtesy of Greg Premru (gregpremru.com).*

Boston Common is the anchor for the Emerald Necklace, a system of connected parks that winds through many of Boston's neighborhoods. With its grand sweep down from the majestic State House, the Common provides an uninterrupted view of green expanse, historic city buildings, and people. It contains walking paths, promenades, a frog pond for skating, play areas, and a war monument. The park hosts concerts, church services, protests, and other sorts of gatherings. Both Martin Luther King, Jr. and Pope John Paul II have made speeches from here. *Courtesy of D. Peter Lund.*

Rob Bramhall Architects

Andover, Massachusetts

Rob Bramhall Architects is a designer of fine custom homes and vacation properties in waterfront, woodland, and mountain settings, as well as in urban and suburban communities throughout the northeast. Based outside of Boston, our small, full-service professional practice is best-known for the architectural and interior design of townhouses, country houses, guesthouses, boathouses, barns, cottages, and outbuildings — even small residential villages, as well as campus, club, resort, and recreation facilities.

A New Englander by birth, I moved west to the mountains of Montana and Wyoming to pursue my professional training. I also studied in Europe, later returning to Boston to apprentice with several large, international firms. Energized by a vision of producing quality architecture in a simpler setting and drawn by the prospect of being able to work at a level of pure passion in direct and purposeful collaboration with my clients, I opened my own practice, which is now celebrating its twenty-first year.

As a designer, my work is inspired by the traditions that have guided architects and builders for generations. It's about quality, simplicity, and balance, thoughtful detailing, and expert craftsmanship. It's about enhancing the natural beauty of the land and creating architecture with a sense of integrity and a lasting presence. It's about environmental sensitivity and sustainability and the discovery and integration of exciting and ever-evolving innovations. However, most importantly, for me and my colleagues, it's about the high standards we hold ourselves to as professionals in terms of going the distance — with passion, energy, and enthusiasm — to get it right for the owners of the places and spaces we help to create.

SALTWATER BARN

Period stonewalls create a foreground for this new home, built on the footprint of an old saltwater farm horse barn.

The house rises gently from the site and is softened with indigenous coastal grasses, flowers, and shrubbery.

Landscaped terraces provide space for outdoor living in warm weather.

A former paddock area in back of the house is landscaped with a swimming pool, pool-house, and generous open space for summer lawn games.

A story-and-a-half ell off the main box of the barn houses a light-filled kitchen and the family sitting area and fireplace.

A glass-enclosed corridor floods the interior with light and links the house with a three-car garage and guest suite.

Designed to function much like an old summer inn, this traditional American Shingle style beach house by Rob Bramhall Architects is nestled into its waterfront site.

A courtyard with a swimming pool provides privacy and protection from the wind off the water.

A landscaped walkway leads from the beach to the private fenced courtyard.

Landscaping on the waterside of the house is natural, with restored dunes and beach grasses.

This new home, designed by Rob Bramhall Architects, is set on a secluded ten-acre parcel of gently sloping farmland and perimeter woodlands. © *Alexander Vertikoff.*

The structure appears to rise organically from a field of hay and wildflowers.

Traditional New England materials, notably red cedar shingle and stone, ground the building within its natural setting. © *Alexander Vertikoff*.

The rugged fieldstone guest suite contrasts with the cedar shingle siding on the main box of the house. Over-scaled windows fill the house with light and frame views out over the expansive meadowlands.

A barn-like ell, with pass-through and cupola, houses a three-car garage and the second floor family game room.

The entry foyer features a vaulted coffered ceiling. © *Alexander Vertikoff.*

When watching the Boston Red Sox, many people like to sit under the Green Monster at Fenway Park. This 36'2" (11.3 m) high left field wall is the highest among current major league baseball fields. The Green Monster prevents home runs that would clear the walls of other ballparks. *Courtesy of Fran Gardino.*

SsD

Cambridge, Massachusetts

SsD has always seen design as an interdisciplinary and collaborative venture. We see the process of sitting down with a client as a way to uncover ways in which minimum form can take maximum effect. Not only does this apply to how a house should take advantage of passive and active environmental strategies, but it also relates to how the spaces are used on a day-to-day basis. By refining our design solution, we have come to believe that it is more important to build smaller and more effectively while not losing sight of the quality of the space itself. Paring down does not have to be an exercise in leading an ascetic life, however. Instead, simplicity in and of itself can be a luxury, a focus on the essential, the sensual, and a heightened awareness of our immediate environment.

In this way, we strive to bridge the utopian and the pragmatic. Why not embrace the optimism of envisioning the way life can be in its most elevated moment? Instead of dreaming of an unlimited budget to achieve our dreams, we look at the design problem from many different angles. For instance, we don't separate aspects of architecture, landscape, history, social systems, and building codes into their individual silos. We are problem solvers and look at all these aspects simultaneously, so that each interrelated discipline symbiotically gains from the other. In this way, sustainability emerges as a naturally integrated result instead of something that is added to project.

BRAVER HOUSE

In many older suburbs, the typical pattern of construction is to replace an existing house with a much larger one built out to the legal setbacks. The Braver House, designed by SsD, is a prototypical alternative: a small, efficient residence that simultaneously minimizes its actual footprint while maximizing its perceived sense of interior space. The combination of the screens and overall massing allows the house to read as a pair of smaller pavilions with landscape in between, rather than one larger building. Replacing the yard within the screens with permeable hardscape drastically reduces the use of potable water. Augmenting this, a rainwater collection system is located at the gutter downspouts.

Expanding the sense of space is achieved by building a diaphanous screen to the setback line, expanding the territory of the interior to the exterior without creating additional conditioned interior space that requires extra energy to heat and cool.

The building shifts in plan as well, re-directing long diagonal views across the side yards instead of short views looking into adjacent yards. A small balcony from the master bedroom allows protected access to the outdoors.

Interior spaces are overlapped with the exterior; the wooden screen becomes a middle ground that defines the expanded space. In the living area, a high efficiency, low-emission wood burning stove supplements the solar-powered radiant floor heating system. Its proximity to the passive ventilation stack directly opposite from it allows heat to be drawn into the upper floors of the house.

A renewable cork floor is used throughout the house and is matched in color to the exterior wooden screen. As the spaces shift in half levels, views extend through the public areas of the house and to the yard beyond.

COULTER HOUSE

An addition above an existing structure expands the experience of the house without physically making it bigger. The heavy inward-looking existing stone ground level is juxtaposed against the light outward-looking new second level.

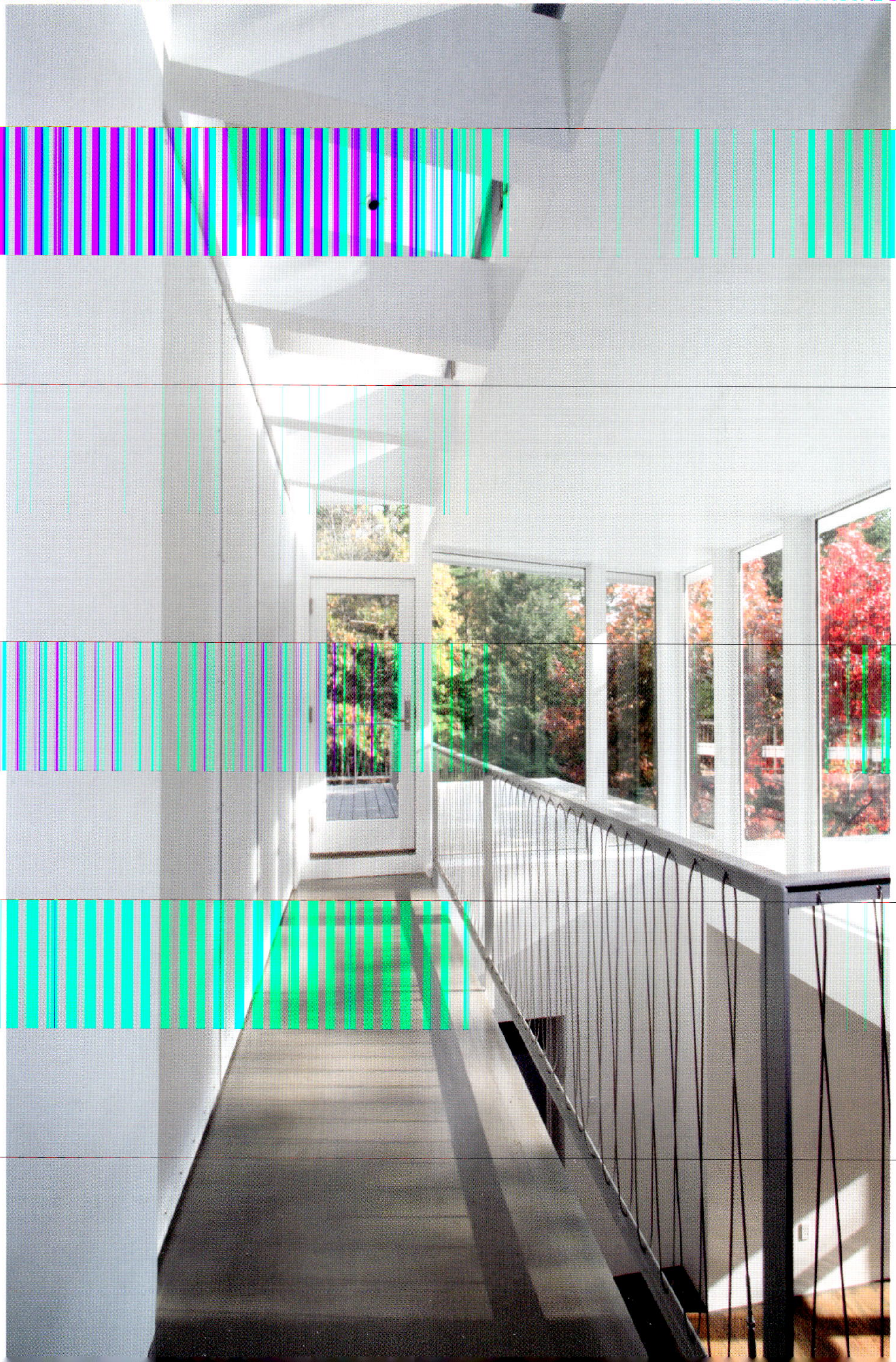

Instead of increasing the size of the house, SsD conceived of the new upper level as three pavilions. The light-filled "seams" between the volumes expand the experience of the spaces.

One of the in-between spaces between the pavilions becomes a captured bamboo courtyard.

Passive solar techniques are used throughout the house: A roof overhang blocks the high summer sun while allowing the low winter sun in. The thermally massive floor remains cool in the summer and warm in the winter.

A strategic cut in the ceiling connects the existing ground floor with the new second floor. Natural light and ventilation is now brought into the once-dark space that required artificial lighting, even during the day.

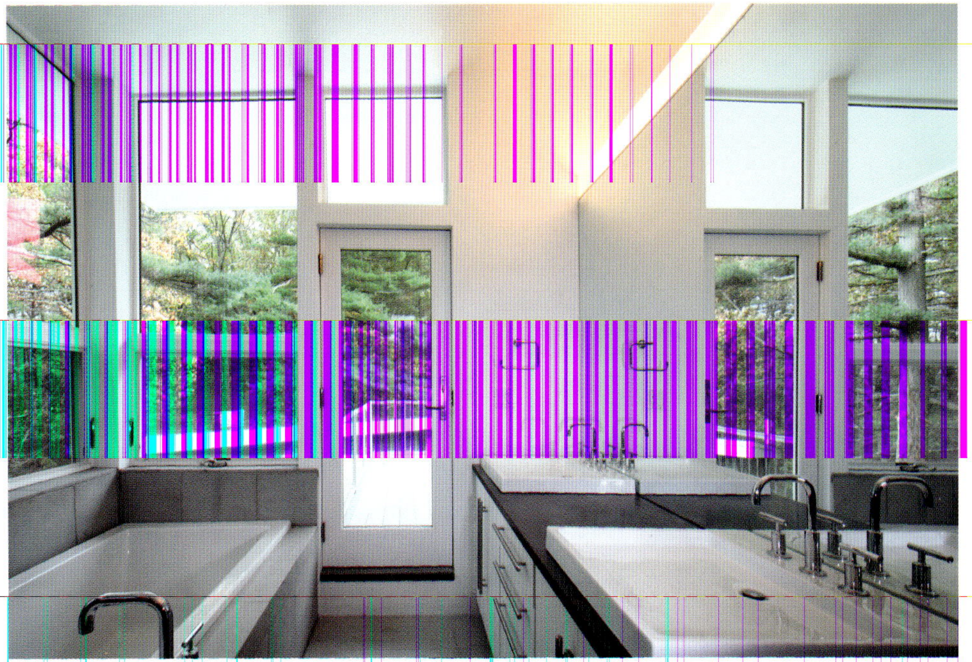

The master bath is level with the trees.

The double height space stack ventilates the house, bringing cool air from below and releasing hot air through upper level clerestory windows. This passive cooling technique eliminates the need for air conditioning.

BIG DIG HOUSE

As a prototype building that demonstrates how infrastructural refuse can be salvaged and reused, the structural system for this house is comprised of steel and concrete discarded from Boston's Big Dig. It utilizes over 600,000 lbs. of salvaged materials from elevated portions of the dismantled I-93 highway in the Commonwealth.

The salvaged highway materials formed the columns, beams, floors, and ceiling of the house. With strategic front-end planning, much needed community programs, including schools, libraries, and housing, could be constructed whenever infrastructure is deconstructed, saving valuable resources, embodied energy, and taxpayer dollars.

SsD created subtle spatial arrangements and light-filled volumes in planning the reassembly of the materials — rather like working with a pre-fab system.

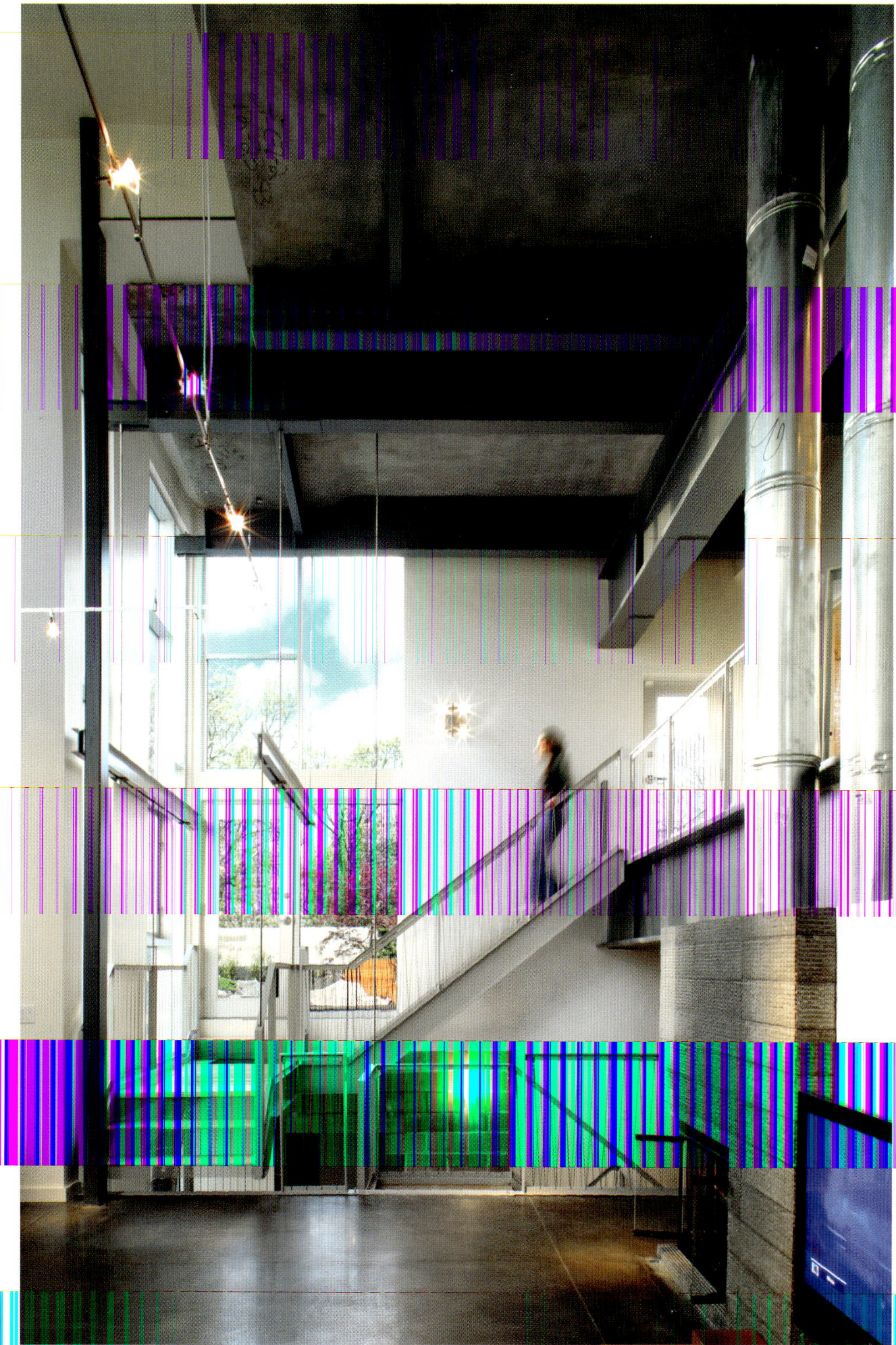

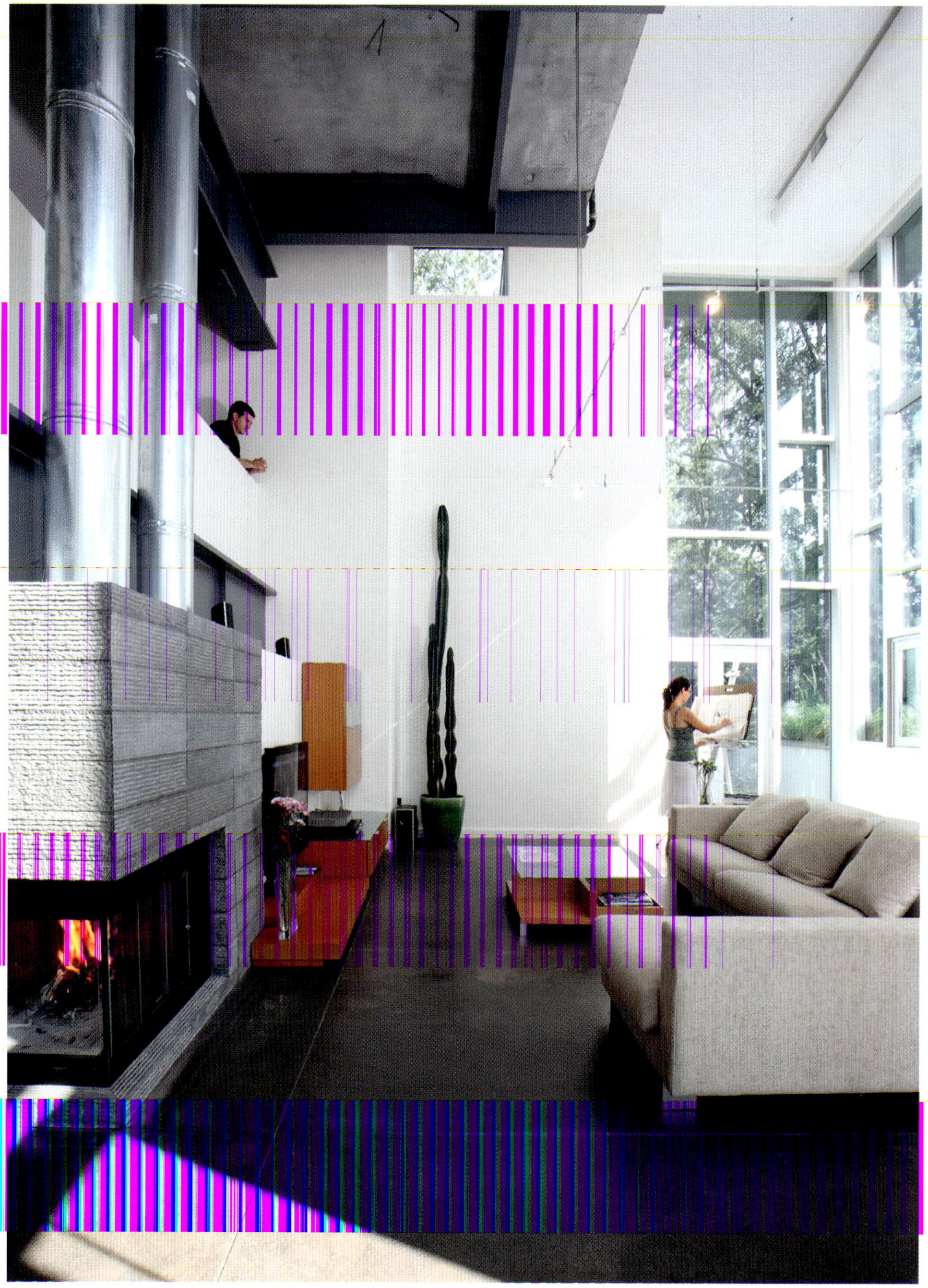

The discarded highway materials were reused in many different ways.

These materials, however, are capable of carrying much higher loads than the standard structure, easily allowing the integration of large-scale roof gardens.

An open stair connects the split levels of the house.

Window walls in conjunction with double height spaces bring natural light deep into the space while exterior overhangs shade summer sun.

The Weld Boathouse, a Harvard-owned building, is a well-known Cambridge landmark just a short walk from Harvard Yard. Situated at the halfway point of the Head of the Charles course, it is over one hundred years old. *Courtesy of Fran Gardino*.

ZeroEnergy Design

Boston, Massachusetts

ZeroEnergy Design (ZED) operates at the intersection of high design and high performance. We are committed to innovative and ecologically sensible designs and believe technical, financial, and aesthetic aspects must be considered holistically.

RENAISSANCE TEAM: Our multidisciplinary design team spans the fields of architecture, engineering, and finance. We use this expertise to take a calculated and iterative approach to designing high performance homes. We employ computer renderings to help clients visualize different design directions and simulate the energy performance of several insulation options to identify the optimal solution, empowering both clients and design team to make informed decisions at every step in the process.

INSPIRED ARCHITECTURE: Inspiration for each design draws upon the surrounding landscape, our collaboration with the client and their environmental ideologies, as well as the challenge of making energy efficiency beautiful. Within our design, we capture an experience; one that blends interaction with view, light, form, and aesthetics. The result is an architecture that is uniquely informed by place, subject, and ideals.

CLIENT ADVOCACY: Our practice of architecture is both a calculated art and service. We articulate designs on our clients' behalf, upholding their objectives and tailoring decisions to their aesthetic preferences, budgetary goals, and environmental ideology. We help the client identify a qualified builder who can deliver quality construction within the project budget, and we advocate for the client throughout construction.

ENERGY & SUSTAINABILITY: We believe that global climate change is the biggest environmental risk we face. Our highest priority is dramatically reducing the energy consumption of our homes, achieved through careful attention to the integrity of the thermal enclosure, well-designed systems, efficient appliances and lighting, as well as renewable energy. Healthy indoor air quality, water-saving strategies, non-toxic materials, and sensitivity to the local site are all vital considerations to each of our designs.

LEED GOLD CERTIFIED RESIDENCE

ZED designed this LEED Gold certified residence to replace an old, deteriorating, summer home. The client's family had traditions rich in visual arts and environmental stewardship. These legacies are reflected in the new home's modern style, energy efficiency, and connection with the outdoor environment. The vibrant red and orange facade colors were inspired by the site's autumnal color palette, while the Cape Cod location influenced the selection of ship lapped cedar siding. *Courtesy of Michael J. Lee.*

The covered porch provides a wonderful outdoor space with protection from the elements. It is the perfect place to be during both harsh sunny days and warm summer rains. *Courtesy of Michael J. Lee.*

A roof deck at the second level of the house offers the wonderful feeling of living in the trees. It has a glass rail to open the view toward the lake and an outdoor kitchen for entertaining. *Courtesy of Michael J. Lee*.

The lakeside deck extends off of the covered porch and has a double step to grade. It provides both a place to sit and eliminates the need for an obtrusive handrail. *Courtesy of Michael J. Lee*.

The entire family loves art and light, both of which are an integral part of the house. ZED provided generous windows, a raised ceiling, and minimal window trim to create a bright airy feeling throughout the living space. *Courtesy of Michael J. Lee.*

In the living space, ZED selected finish materials with durability, low maintenance, and, of course, with aesthetics in mind. Well-traveled paths are delineated in durable travertine tile, while the remaining living spaces feature bamboo flooring. The quartz kitchen countertop rests on custom maple cabinets, which were treated with a low-VOC stain to match an antique family heirloom. Julia Child-inspired open shelves were a client request and offer quick access to dishware. The generous counter space provides ample working area for food prep, seating for everyday use, and a built-in wine rack to cradle each vintage.

The pantry cabinets are located near the entry. We recessed the cabinets deep into the wall and matched them with the base kitchen cabinets to tie the space and use together. This allows the wall, running from the entry to the lakeside deck, to read as one, as opposed to a series of segmented pieces. The result is a clean, expansive working space with friendly aesthetics and abundant storage to meet the needs of any chef. *Courtesy of Michael J. Lee.*

Abutting the roof deck is a lush, living green roof, built to fill the view with vegetation at eye level while seated. Although it is primarily a design feature, the green roof reduces storm water runoff. Solar electric panels rest atop the second floor roof and offset thirty percent of the annual electricity use. *Courtesy of Michael J. Lee*.

This private retreat and vacation residence is located in a beautiful community on the Rhode Island coast. The home bundles high performance and efficient use of space in a small package. The client sought a two-bedroom, two-bath home that was rightly sized for their family and minimized the amount of energy used — nothing more, nothing less. ZED designed a sleek, simple, gable roofed structure and proposed the Passive House standard, which is a building performance standard that yields an extremely low-energy home. A combination of exceptional insulation, air sealing, high performance windows, and solar gain reduces the space conditioning requirements to a mere fraction of a typical home, which means only a small heating system is needed for both the energy savings and the increased comfort. The house is pending final Passive House certification. *Courtesy of Greg Premru (gregpremru.com)*.

Despite the modest footprint, the home addresses all of the client's needs. Its efficient space planning features storage space and a loft area above. The loft provides the children with a private place to spend time away from the adults. *Courtesy of Greg Premru (gregpremru.com)*.

The open floor plan of the living and dining areas features a dining nook that bumps out of the southern side and a mobile kitchen island for complete flexibility. *Courtesy of Greg Premru (gregpremru.com)*.

The client also expressed their love of baths. ZED included a dedicated sun-filled tub room in the southeast corner of the home adjacent to the master bath. *Courtesy of Greg Premru (gregpremru.com).*

Zed carefully designed this modern, high-performance house, situated on a coastal bank 115 feet above the surrounding bay, to seize the site opportunities. The two shifting volumes of the house appear to drift within the coastal topography, each form expanding toward the ocean. *Courtesy of © Eric Roth.*

The home was designed with environmentally sound principles that minimize its water use, feature native landscaping, and gets nearly seventy-five percent of its energy from renewable sources, including a roof-mounted solar array. The house features a super-insulated building envelope, durable finishes inside and out, a geothermal heating and cooling system, radiant heating, a solar electric system, and fresh air ventilation, which ensures healthy indoor air quality. *Courtesy of © Eric Roth.*

Inside the living space, the tapered roof plane slopes up and out toward the view, drawing the eye outside, while the glazing draws the horizon in, inviting the ocean to complete the dynamic fourth wall of the space. The glazing asymmetrically wraps and exposes the corner of the interior living space, bringing in light and capturing the majestic ocean view. *Courtesy of © Eric Roth*.

The super-insulated wall of the living space opens to expose its depth, revealing a framed view of the dining room and four niches carved out for book storage. These horizontal lines and orthogonal forms continue in the bench beneath, beside the fireplace, and in the linear fluorescent light fixtures. These horizontal reference lines extend out through the expansive windows to the true ocean horizon and back into the space. *Courtesy of © Eric Roth.*

The kitchen is the social epicenter of the living space. The generously sized island permits simultaneous social gathering and functional food prep space. The chef's commanding view includes not only the ocean but also the surrounding layers of activity: the dining room, the living space, the outside patio, and the roof plane to connect them all. The social gatherers enjoy the activity at the kitchen island; the entertainment side of the island provides space for seating and access to the wine refrigerator, while the functional side is left to the chef. *Courtesy of © Eric Roth.*

The wood roof and floor planes create warm ambiance throughout the home, as ample transom windows provide constant daylight. The dining area also takes advantage of the exceptional ocean view. *Courtesy of © Eric Roth.*

When night falls, the house illuminates the sky.
Courtesy of © Eric Roth.

Boston skyline view. Note the Massachusetts State House with its gilded dome. Samuel Adams and Paul Revere laid its cornerstone on July 4, 1795, making it the oldest existing building on Beacon Hill. Revere also provided nails and copper for the construction of the dome. Completed by January 1798, the building and grounds cover two city blocks. Paul Revere covered the dome in copper in 1802. At its peak, Bulfinch placed a gilt pinecone to symbolize the forests that made it possible for the early settlers to survive. The dome was gilded in 23-karat gold leaf in 1874. Widely acclaimed as one of the more magnificent and well-situated buildings in the country, the State House dome dominated the Boston skyline until the advent of the skyscraper. It has served as a model for the U. S. Capitol Building and other state capitals. *Courtesy of Harry Taplin.*

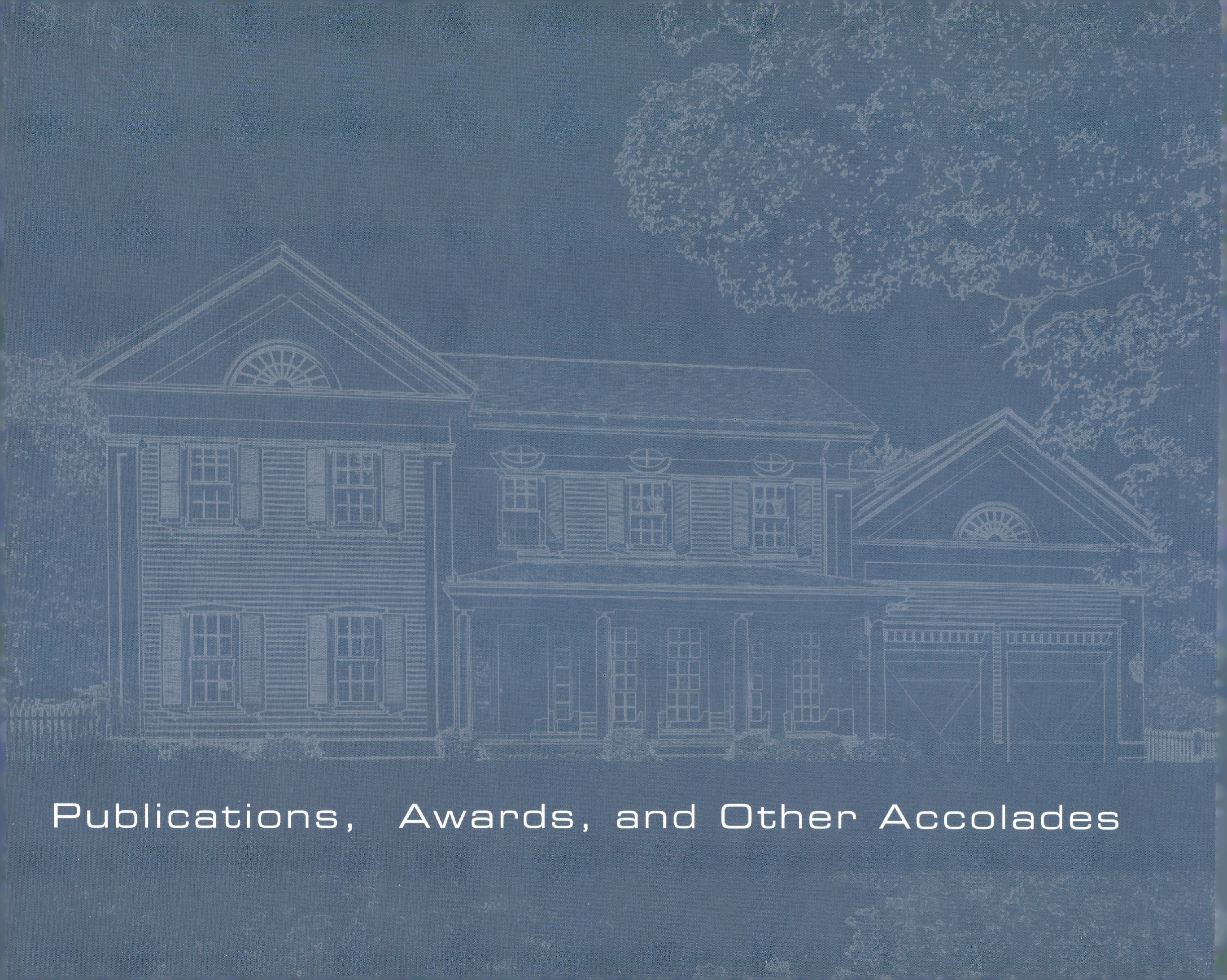

Publications, Awards, and Other Accolades

Bechtel Frank Erickson Architects

Bernier, Nicole. "Pared Up, Pared Down," *Boston Magazine*, March 1998. Subject: Marshall-Salwen residence.

Bernstein, Fred. "Boston Uncommon," *Metropolitan Homes*, September/October 1998. Subject: Renovation.

Crosbie, Michael J. *Houses Of God, Religious Architecture for a New Millennium*. Mulgrave Victoria, Australia: Images Publishing, 2006. Subject: House of Prayer Lutheran Church.

Storrs, Francis. "One Year, One House," *Boston HOME Magazine*, Fall 2009. Subject: Renovated English Cottage.

This Old House Magazine. November/December 1997. Companion to the autumn 1997 *This Old House Series*. Subject: Milton House and Norm's Workshop.

This Old House Magazine. Spring 1998, Collector Edition to Television Series. Subject: The Milton Project, Renovating a Classic Colonial.

Yee, Roger. "Fire Walker," *Contract Design*, January 1997; New Faces of 1997. Subject: Malden Mills Headquarters.

Catalano Architects

Bermar, Amy. "Architects Called Upon to Add Sales Appeal," *Boston Globe Magazine*, March 1996.

Bodah, Paula M. "Quiet Elegance," *New England Home's Cape & Islands*, Summer 2009.

Book, Jeff. "Top Flights," *Departures*, March/April 1999.

Borseti, Teri. "Man's Return to the Cave," *Boston Common*, October/November 2010.

Brosnan, Michael. "Gerrish Island Retreat," *Down East Magazine*, February 1990.

Cole, Regina. "Learning Curve," *Design New England*, November/December 2008.

"The Finishing Touch," *New England Home's Cape & Islands*, Summer 2008.

Connors, Jill. "At the Water's Edge: A Summer House on Cape Cod's Southern Shore Recalls the Grand Estates of a Bygone Era," *Design New England*, July/August 2009.

Cunningham, Caroline. "Wayland's Wild West," *Boston Common*, Holiday 2007.

Fine Homebuilding Kitchens & Baths, Fall/Winter 2007.

Gehrman, Elizabeth. "Coming Home," *Boston Globe Magazine*, January 24, 2010.

Goldberger, Paul. "Beyond the Master's Voice," *New York Times Magazine*, 1993.

Grauerholz, Mary. "From Counters to Cookers," *Cape Cod Islands Home*, Holiday 2009.

Henry, Saxon. "New England Water Color," *Home Magazine*, September 2002.

Hogeland, Jennifer. "Sustaining New England," *Green Building & Design Magazine*, November 2010.

Howley, Kathleen. "Double the Pleasure," *Boston Globe Magazine*, May 7, 2000.

"Intelligence Gathering," *Custom Home*, January/February 2003.

Jordan, Mary Beth. "Our Son the Architect," *Metropolitan Home*, March 1989.

Keith, Todd. "Second Chance," *Better Homes & Gardens' Beautiful New Homes*, Summer 2009.

Kleinman, Susan. "Building on Tradition," *Home Magazine*, April 2002.

O'Brien, Greg. "Pleasant Surprises," *Cape Cod & Islands Home*, Summer 2007.

Oberoi, Michele. "A Taste of the Good Life," *Upscale Living Magazine*, Winter 2007.

Pittel, Christine. "Flying Colors," *House Beautiful*, July 2004.

Sieberling Pond, Catherine. "A World of Difference," *New England Home* (cover of premiere issue), September/October 2005.

"Simply Stylish." *Dream Kitchens*, Vol. 3, No. 1, 2006.

Sinnett, Molly Reid. "Traditional Light," *Better Homes & Gardens' Beautiful New Homes*, Fall 2002.

Slack, Steve. "Island Idyll: A Perfect Summer Getaway on Nantucket Island," *Renovation Style*, June/July 2001.

Strohm, Kimberlee. "All the Comforts of Home," *Cape Cod Islands Home*, Annual 2002.

"Strokes of Brilliance," *Cape Cod Islands & Home*, Holiday 2006.

Sutton, Linda. "Coastal Character," *Elegant Homes*, Fall/Winter 2010.

Sutton, Tina. "The Tone Sets the Tone," *Boston Globe Magazine*, February 12, 2006.

"Sweeping Shingle." *Custom Home*, September/October 1996.

Trends, *Home & Architectural*, Vol. 15, No. 4, 1999.

Trends, *Home & Architectural*, Vol. 16, No. 4, 2000.

Trends, *Home & Architectural*, Vol. 19, No. 4, 2003.

"Vanity Fair," *Cape Cod & Islands Home*, Spring 2007.

Winzenried, Rebecca. "The Children's Library," *Home Magazine*, September 2001.

Awards

Custom Home Design Grand Award, 1996.

New England Design Inductee, Thomas P. Catalano, 2011.

Charles Rose Architects Inc.

Aronson, Steven A. L. "Joshua Bell: Orchestrating a Penthouse in New York for the Virtuoso Violinist." *Architectural Digest*, May 2010; pp.110-115.

Beaver, Robyn ed. *100 More of the World's Best Houses*. Mulgrave Victoria, Australia: The Images Publishing Group Pty Ltd., 2005; pp. 82-85, 256-259.

Rose, Charles. *Architect*. New York, New York: Princeton Architectural Press, 2006.

Vassallo, Marc. *The Barefoot Home*. Newton, Connecticut: The Taunton Press, Inc. 2006; pp. 62-69.

David Sharff

"Balancing Act," *Design New England*, January/February 2011.

"Child's Play," *Design New England*, November/ December 2009.

"Sketch Pad," *New England Home*, September/October 2010.

Valigursky, Michelle and Vail, Lisa. *Creating Curb Appeal*. Atglen, Pennsylvania: Schiffer Publishing, 2009.

Awards

Single family home design, Habitat for Humanity, 2010.

Eck/MacNeely Architects

Eck, Jeremiah. *The Distinctive Home: A Vision of Timeless Design*. Newton, Connecticut: Taunton Press, 2004.

The Face of Home: A New Way to Look at the Outside of Your Home. Newton, Connecticut: Taunton Press, 2006.

House in the Landscape: Siting Your Home Naturally. New York, New York: Princeton Architectural Press, 2010.

Feinmann Inc.

"Metamorphosis of a Butler's Kitchen," *Distinctive Kitchens*, #47, pp. 30-31.

CHEF'S KITCHEN

Boston Globe Magazine Special Issue: Your Home, June 12, 2005. pp. 79-81.

Distinctive Kitchens, #34, pp. 20-23.

Renovation Trends, Vol. 22, No. 12, pp. 100-105.

Robb Report Luxury Home, Winter 2005, pp. 34-35.

Awards

2005 Prism Gold Award for Best Kitchen over $250,000.

2005 Best of the Best Northeast Design Award for Kitchen Transformation.

2005 Luxury Living Platinum Award for Best Kitchen.

2005 Luxury Living Best in Show Award.

ASIAN INSPIRATION

Distinctive Design New England, September 2007.

NECN Dream House, September 2007.

Rooney, Ashley. *Asian Influence on Architecture and Design*. Atglen, Pennsylvania: Schiffer Publishing, 2010.

Awards

2007 Prism Gold Award for Renovation/Addition under $250,000.

2007 Best of the Best Design Award for Addition under $250,000.

VICTORIAN RE-ENVISIONED

Distinctive Design New England, September 2007.

NECN Dream House, June 2006.

Awards

2005 Chrysalis Award for Best Whole House Design & Renovation over $250,000.

2005 Professional Remodeler Best of the Best Award for Private Residence.

2006 Luxury Living Platinum Award for Whole House Remodel.

Gleysteen Design

"Gleysteen Design, LLC: Eye-Catching Design Concepts Span Many Schools of Architecture," *Luxury Home Quarterly*, January/February 2011; article featuring the Ridge House and the Overlook House.

OVERLOOK

"Night and Day," *Boston Globe Magazine* (cover story), February 20, 2011.

RIDGE

"Curve Appeal," *The Boston Globe Magazine* (cover story), September 11, 2005.
"Modern Masterpiece," *Accent Home & Garden* (cover), January/February 2008.
"North Shore Folly," *Metropolitan Home*, Fall 2008; article featuring the Ridge House garage.
Trends Very Best Kitchen and Bathrooms. New York, New York: Time Home Entertainment, 2006; pp. 168-173.

SANDY POND

"Change of Space," *Boston Home Magazine*, Summer 2009.
"Two Many Cooks," *Design New England*, March/April 2008.

MID-CENTURY MODERN

"Modern Makeover," *New England Home*, November/December 2009.

AWARDS

Clarke Kitchen Design Awards. First place for Contemporary Kitchen, 2011.

OTHER

"2007 Coastal Living Idea House," *Coastal Living Magazine*, 2007; Portsmouth, Rhode Island residence.
"A Federal Case," *New England Home*, September/October 2005; Newport, Rhode Island residence.
"An Exclusive Showcase of New England's Finest Architects," *Dream Homes New England*, 2008. pp. 98-103.
Architectural Digest, December 2008; vignette featuring Ridge Ho.
"Child's Play," *Renovation Style Magazine*, Spring 2005; Weston, Massachusetts residence.
"Let There Be Light," *The Boston Globe Magazine*, August 2004; Lincoln, Massachusetts residence.
"Make it Personal." *Design New England*, May/June 2008; Brookline, Massachusetts residence.
"Reshaping the Familiar," *Better Homes and Gardens: Beautiful Homes*, Spring 2007; Weston, Massachusetts residence.
Rooney, Ashley. *Shingle Style Architecture for the 21st Century*. Atglen, Pennsylvania: Schiffer Publishing, 2008; multiple Gleysteen Design projects.
"Traditional Outside, Modern Inside," *Yankee Magazine*, September 2005; Weston, Massachusetts residence.

Höweler+Yoon

Cullerton, Eric, editor. *Young Architects Americas*. Colognei, Germany: DAAB, 2007.
"emBodied Tectonics." *Material Process: Young Architects 4*. New York, New York: Princeton Architectural Press, 2003, pp. 124-149.
Galindo, Michelle. *1000x Architecture of the Americas*. Switzerland: Braun Verlag, 2008.
Höweler, Eric and Meejin Yoon. *Expanded Practice: Höweler + Yoon Architecture/My Studio*. New York, New York: Princeton Architectural Press. 2009; p. 208.
Murray, Hubert. "The New Establishment Meets the Next Wave," *Architectural Record*, May 2008.
Weisstuch, Liza. "Thinking Outside and Inside the Box," *The Boston Globe*, May 15, 2008.
Yoon, Meejin and Meredith Miller, editors. *Public Works: Unsolicited Small Projects for the Big Dig*. New York, New York: MAP Book, 2008.

AWARDS

Architectural Record's Design Vanguard, 2007.
Architecture League's Emerging Voices Award, 2007.
Athena Award, RISD/Target Emerging Designer Award, 2008.
Boston Society of Architects Honor Awards for Design Excellence for "Low-Rez Hi-Fi," 2007.
Residential Architect Magazine Merit Award for "Outside-In Loft," 2008.

H. P. Rovinelli Architects

Carabet, Brian G. and John A. Shand. *Dream Homes New England*. Plano, Texas: Panache Partners, LLC, 2008.

Hamilton, William L. "New Art and Craft of the Kitchen," *The New York Times*, May 29, 1997.

Healey, Jane. "Kitchen Matters," *Boston Magazine's Home & Garden*, Spring 2005; Boston Magazine Publications, Editor: Emily McManus. Vol. 3, No. 1, pp. 84-85, 119-120.

O'Connell, John. "The Politics of Good Design," *Boston Spirit Magazine* (David Zimmerman), July/August 2010; Editor: James A. Lopata. Vol. 6, No. 4, pp. 60-65.

Snoonian, Deborah. "All the Right Rooms," *This Old House Magazine* (Charles R. Kammerer), January/ February 2010; Editor: Scott Omelianuk, pp.72-79.

Waldbieser, Jill and Janine White, editors. *Boston Magazine's Home & Garden*, Spring 2007; Boston Magazine Publications, Vol. 5, No. 1, pp. 106-113, 140-141.

Jan Gleysteen Architects

Carabet, Brian G., and John A. Shand. *Dream Homes New England*. Malaysia: Panache Partners, 2008.

Awards

2011 Dream Home Award for "Best Custom Home Over 9000 SF."

Boston's 2011 Bulfinch Award for "Best Suburban Residence."

Boston's 2011 Prism Award for "Best Single Family Home."

Jonathan Levi Architects

Baumann, James. "The 21st Century Project Design Showcase: The Home," *flexDorm Design Concept*, 2007; pp.14-23.

Biemiller, Lawrence. "The Dorm Room of the Future," *flexDorm Design Concept: The Chronicle of Higher Education*, February 23, 2007; pp. B12-B13.

Brake, Alan. "Competition Rethinks Student Housing for the Echo-Boom Generation," *flexDorm Design Concept: Architectural Record*, April 2007; p. 40 of Chicago catalog, cover. Brookline Residence: Wohnungen in Hozbauweise, Dieter.

Branch, M. A. "Jonathan Levi's Wood Detailing – Rethinking the Wood House." *Progressive Architecture*, May 1994; pp. 70-75.

Devido, Alfred. "Auburn Court/Chestnut Hill Residence: House Design." *Art and Practice*. New York, New York: John Wiley & Sons, 1996; pp,. 76-77, 104-105.

Eck, Jeremiah. "Brookline and May Residences." *The Distinctive Home: A Vision of Timeless Design*. Newtown, Connecticut: The Taunton Press, 2003; pp. 66, 157.

Herzog, Thomas et al. "Patent Windows." *Façade Construction Manual*. Basel, Switzerland: Birkhauser Architecture, 2004. p. 131.

Levinson, Nancy. "Harvard Graduate Student Housing." *Architectural Record*, December 2004, pp. 177, 186-191.

Ojeda, O. R. "Brookline Residence." *The New American House*. New York, New York: Whitney Library of Design, 1995; pp. 196-203.

Practice, Jonathan. "Portfolio: Auburn Court/Low-Cost Rural Housing Emerging" and "Portfolio: Brookline Residence/Chestnut Hill Residence," *Progressive Architecture*. Hoboken, New Jersey: John Wiley & Sons, 1996; pp. 76-77, 104-105.

Russell, J. S. "The Southgate Building: The End of Dumb Walls," *Architectural Record*, October 1993; pp. 109, 114-115.

Vidiella, Àlex Sánchez. "May Residence." *The Sourcebook of Contemporary Architecture*. Barcelona, Spain: Collins Design and Loft Publications, 2007; pp. 494-501.

Kelly Monnahan Design

Addison, Windrum, "Truro Contemporary," *Cape Cod and Island Home*, Autumn 2009.

Bernstein, Fred A. "The Feeling is Neutral," *Metropolitan Home Magazine*, September 2006.
"Second Nature," *Metropolitan Home Magazine*, November 2006.

Hammatt, Heather, "Vintage Views," *Landscape Architecture Magazine*, November 2004.

Hoard, Flanery. "Small Perks," *Metropolitan Home Magazine*, January/February 2009.

Lassell, Michael. *Metropolitan Home Design 100: The Last Word on Modern Interiors*. Boston, Massachusetts: Hachette Filipacchi Media, 2010.
Metropolitan Home, Glamour: Making it Modern. Boston, Massachusetts: Hachette Filipacchi Media, 2009.

Levitt, Rachel. "Bathing Beauty," *Boston Home Magazine*, Fall 2010.
"Best Modern Architect, 2011," *Boston Home Magazine*, Winter 2011.
"Modern Influences," *Boston Magazine*, April 2010.
"Neighbors, Same Building Different Space," *Boston Home Magazine*, Winter 2009.

Molvar, Kari." A Modern View," *Boston Magazine*, July 2004.

O'Connor, John T. "Living with Art, Shock of The New," *Esplanade Magazine*, November/December 2010.

Padilla, Magan (Jury Panel). "New England Charm," *Garden Design Magazine*, September/October 2010.

Padjen, Elizabeth S. (Jury Panel). "Cape Cod Residence," *Architecture Boston*, January-February 2004.

Young, Lucie. "Capelight," *Metropolitan Home Magazine*. July-August 2003.

Margolis Inc.

"Cabrini Green Master Plan Illustrations," *Architectural Record*, September 1997.

Dream Homes: New England. Piano, Texas: Panache Partners, LLC, 2008.

Gartner, Marieke Cassia. "Ocean Panorama," *Period Homes*, March 2005.

Gerrie, Anthea. "Having A Ball," *25 Beautiful Homes, British*, June 2003.

"Real Homes Abroad," *25 Beautiful Homes, British*, December 2002-January 2003.

"Ocean View," *25 Beautiful Homes, British*, October 2002.

"Real Homes Abroad," *Real Homes Magazine*, December 2002-January 2003.

Guralnick, Estelle. "Orange Crush," *The Boston Globe Magazine*, September 20, 2009.

Hayday, Andrea. "Fresh Perspective," *Remodel Magazine*, September 2010.

Maton, Sally. "A Boston Tea Party," *Everything America*, August/September 2004.

"The White House," *Everything America*, December 2004/January 2005.

Miller, Margo. "At Home: Light Fantastic," *The Boston Globe*, May 21, 1998.

"Water's Edge," *The Boston Globe*, October 25, 1999.

Awards

AIA Award for Urban Design, 2001: "A Civic Vision for Turnpike Air Rights in Boston." (Illustrations produced in collaboration with Goody, Clancy & Associates).

Trustees of Reservation, Castle Hill: The Inn at Castle Hill Designer Show House Program, 2000.

Maryann Thompson Architects

1000x Landscape Architecture. Germany, Berlin: Verlaghaus Braun, 2009.

Campbell, Robert. "In this Spacious House, You're Always at One with Nature," *The Boston Globe*, January 26, 2006.

Eck, Jeremiah. *House in the Landscape*. New York, New York: Princeton Architectural Press, 2011.

Galindo, Michelle. *1000x Architecture of the Americas*. Germany, Berlin: Verlaghaus Braun, 2008

Ji-Hyun. *New Space 10: Education & Culture*. Seoul, Korea: Archiworld Co., Ltd., 2009.

Meyer & Meyer

"Bali High," *Design New England Magazine*, September/October 2008.

"Best of Boston Home 2011 Interiors," *Boston Home Magazine*, Winter 2011.

"Child's Play," *New England Home Magazine*, May/June 2008.

"Classical Home of the Year," *Hab-i-ta-tion Design Magazine*, June/July 2010.

"Drawn to Tale," *Boston Common Magazine*, Spring 2010.

"In Harmony," *Boston Common Magazine*, Spring 2011.

"Into the Deep," *The Boston Globe Magazine*, September 2010.

"Meet the Architects," *New England Home Magazine*, November/December 2008.

"Meet the Design Professionals," *New England Home Magazine*, September/October 2008.

"Meet the Designer," *New England Home Magazine*, 2006, 2007.

"Particular Passions," *Design New England Magazine*, November/December 2008.

"Penthouse Kitchen by Luxury Kitchens," *Architectural Digest*, April 2009.

"Private Upgrades, The University Club of Boston," *Boston Business Journal*, April 11-17, 2008.

"Providence Group looks proudly at their rehab on Newbury Street," *The Back Bay Sun*, November 30, 2007.

"Public Living Quarters: Designing for Durability and Homey Feel," *The Back Bay Sun*, November 9, 2007.

"Shared History," *Boston Home Magazine*, Spring 2010.

"Sketch Pad, Design Ideas in the Making," *New England Home Magazine*, September/October 2009.

"The Gold Standard" and "Meet the Designer," *New England Home Magazine*, May/June 2007.

Awards

1989: HUD Award for Excellence in Housing and Urban Development: Lowell Housing Authority. New England Regional Council Design Award: JFK/UMass Station Modernization.

1997: National BOMA Award for Best Suburban Office Park: Edgewater Office Park, Wakefield, Massachusetts.

2006: Luxury Living Awards – Gold Award – Most Beautiful Whole House Remodel.

2006 and 2007: PRISM Awards/The Builders Association of Greater Boston.

2009: Best of Boston – Architecture.

2009: PRISM Awards/The Builders Association of Greater Boston.

2010: Classical Home of the Year – Dream Home Awards for English Rose Estate.

2011: Best of Boston Home – Interiors Restoration
• Accessible Design in Public Architecture, Historic Renovation – Monastery of St. Clare, Boston, Massachusetts.
• Best Bathroom Remodeling – Luxury, Best Remodeling/Restoration Over $500,000.
• Best Single-Family Design: Over 5,000 SF.
• Gold Award – 'Creative/Unique' Use of Space.
• Gold Award – 'Best Renovation/Restoration' over $500,000.
• Gold Award - Best Bathroom Remodel, Silver Award – Best Kitchen Remodel.

2011: Illuminating Engineering Society of North America – NYNEX Headquarters, Boston, Massachusetts.

2011: National Terrazzo & Mosaic Association – Armand P. Mercier Community Center, Lowell, Massachusetts.

2011: Preservation Trust Award – Old North Main Street Fire Station, Springfield, Massachusetts.

Moskow Linn Architects, Inc.

MVII

"Fun in the Sun," *Trends*, 2006.

"Honor Awards for Design Excellence," *Architecture Boston*, 2006.

"Martha's Vineyard," *Contemporary Living*. New York, New York: Monacelli Press, 2010.

"New Sustainable Homes," *Collins Design*, 2006.

"Summer Solace, a Vineyard House Soothes with a Japanese Spirit," *Boston Globe Magazine*, 2006.

"When a Lot is Just Enough," *Cape Cod and Islands Home*, 2008.

RESERVOIR HOUSE

"Barn Again," *Design New England*, 2011.

Awards

2010: The U.S. Green Building Council, LEED Certification.

ARBOR HOUSE

"American Idyll," *Metropolitan Home*, 2006.

"Boat Fishes & Vineyards," *Metalmag*, 2005.

Cape Cod Cottage. New York, New York: Princeton Architectural Press, 2006.

"Going For the Green," *Cape Cod View*, 2006.

"Honor Awards for Design Excellence," *Architecture Boston*, 2006.

"In and Up," *Cape Cod Magazine*, 2006.

"Martha's Vineyard is a Showplace for New Domestic Architecture," *The Providence Sunday Journal*, 2005.

"New Sustainable Homes," *Collins Design*, 2006.

"No Dish Towels Needed." *Fine Homebuilding*, 2007.

"Sun Catcher," *Residential Architect*, 2005.

"The Green House," *Boston Home and Garden*, 2006.

The Houses of Martha's Vineyard. New York, New York: Monacelli Press, 2005.

Awards

2005: Boston Society of Architects, Honor Award, Design Excellence.
Cape Cod Magazine, Architectural Design Competition Winner.
Custom Home, Design Honor Awards Merit Citation.

2006: American Institute of Architects Honor Award for Design, Small Projects.

SsD

Bell, Jonathan and Elli Stathaki. *The New Modern House: Redefining Functionalism*. London, England: Kings Road Publishing, 2010.

Campbell, Robert. "Thinking Green, Going Global," *The Boston Globe*, March 15, 2009.

Gardener, Virginia. "Beantown Dream," *Dwell Magazine*, October/November 2004.

Goldberger, Paul. "Salvage Artists," *The New Yorker*, March 19, 2007.

Serifman, Susanna. *Modern Shoestring: Contemporary Architecture on a Budget*. New York, New York: Monicelli Press, 2008.

ZeroEnergy Design

Cole, Regina. "The Green House Effect," *Ocean Home*, July/August 2010; pp. 23-24.

Geronemus, Hillary. "Going Greener," *Boston Home Magazine*, Spring 2010; pp. 54-55.

Hutchins, Shelley D. "2010 EcoHome Design Awards," *EcoHome Magazine*, Summer 2010; pp. 24-25.

Irving, Bruce. "The new New World," *Design New England*, July/August 2009; pp. 70-77.

Marvin, Erin. "Tomorrow's Design Stars," *New England Home*, September/October 2010; pp. 67-85.

Pontolilo, Brian. "Master Bath Floats Anew," *Fine Homebuilding*, Fall/Winter 2010; pp. 36-37.

Awards

2010: Boston Society of Architects | Citation for Sustainability.

- EcoHome Design Awards|Grand Award for Truro Residence.
- Excellence in Design Awards | Finalist.
- LEED Gold for Homes | English Residence, Cape Cod.
- New England Home Magazine | 5 Under 40 Award.
- Sub-Zero Wolf Kitchen Design Contest | Regional Winner.
- USGBC Natural Talent Design Competition | Winner.

2011: Best of Boston Home | Best Green Architect

- Perspective in Design Awards | Best New Construction.
- Green Business Award | City of Boston.
- EcoHome Design Awards | Merit Award, Concord Residence.

Contact Information

Bechtel Frank Erickson Architects
1840 Massachusetts Avenue, # 2
Lexington, MA 02420
781.862.3313
www.bfearc.com
info@bfearc.com
www.facebook.com/bfearc

Cambridge Seven Associates
1050 Massachusetts Avenue
Cambridge, MA 02138
617.492.7000
www.c7a.com

Catalano Architects, Inc.
115 Broad Street, 2nd floor
Boston, MA 02110
617.338.7447 x 25
www.catalanoinc.com
tcat@catalanoinc.com

Charles Rose Architects
115 Willow Avenue
Somerville, MA 02144
617.628.5033
www.charlesrosearchitects.com

David Sharff Architect, P.C.
67 West Street
Medfield, MA 02052
508.359.5737
www.davidsharffarchitect.com
david@davidsharffarchitect.com

Eck/MacNeely Architects
560 Harrison Avenue, Suite 403
Boston, MA 02118
617.367.9696
www.eckmacneely.com
jeremiah@eckmacneely.com

Feinmann, Inc.
27 Muzzey Street
Lexington, MA 02421
781.860.9800
www.feinmann.com

Gleysteen Design
185 Mt. Auburn Street
Cambridge, MA 02138
617.492.6060
www.gleysteendesign.com

Höweler+Yoon Architecture
150 Lincoln Street, 3A
Boston, MA 02111
617.517.4101
www.hyarchitecture.com

H. P. Rovinelli Architects
45 Newbury Street, No. 505
Boston, MA 02116
617.236.1770
www.hprovinelli.com

Jan Gleysteen Architects
888 Worcester Street, # 60
Wellesley, MA 02482
781.431.0080
www.jangleysteeninc.com

Jonathan Levi Architects
266 Beacon Street, Suite 3
Boston, MA 02116
617.437.9458
www.leviarc.com
ktanfield@leviarc.com

Kelly Monnahan Design
535 Albany Street, Suite 5A
Boston, MA 02118
617.778.6475
www.kellymonnahan.com
kelly@kellymonnahan.com

LDa Architecture & Interiors
222 Third Street, Suite 3212
Cambridge, MA 02142
617.621.1455
www.LDa-Architects.com
info@LDa-Architects.com

Margolis, Inc.
719 Hale Street
Beverly, MA 01915
978.922.4440
www.margolisinc.com

Maryann Thompson Architects
14 Hillside Avenue
Cambridge, MA 02140
617.491.4144
www.maryannthompson.com
maryann@maryannthompson.com

Meyer & Meyer
396 Commonwealth Avenue
Boston, MA 02215
617.266.0555
www.meyerandmeyerarchitects.com

Moskow Linn Architects, Inc.
88 Broad Street
Boston, MA 02110
617.292.2000 x 28
www.moskowarchitects.com
km@moskowlinn.com

Rob Bramhall Architects
14 Park Street
Andover, MA 01810
978.749.3663
www.robbramhallarchitects.com

SsD
171 Brookline Street
Cambridge, MA 02139
617.576.9300
www.ssdarchitecture.com
info@ssdarchitecture.com

ZeroEnergy Design
156 Milk Street, Suite 3
Boston, MA 02109
617.720.5002 x 102
www.ZeroEnergy.com

BOSTON-BASED PHOTOGRAPHERS

D. Peter Lund

Eleanor Lund

Fran Gardino
www.frangardino.com

Harry Taplin
hltaplin@comcast.net

Walter Harrington
wsharrington@comcast.net

Index